To Graham

Happy Birthday !

hope this helps land the

from

Phil

SALMON FISHING
In Search of Silver

Salmon Fishing

◆

In Search of Silver

John Bailey

The Crowood Press

First published in 1994 by
The Crowood Press Ltd
Ramsbury, Marlborough
Wiltshire SN8 2HR

British Library Cataloguing-in-Publication Data
A catalogue record for this book is available from the British Library.

ISBN 1 85223 790 2

Picture credits
Line-drawings by P. Groombridge.
Photographs by the author.

Phototypeset by Intype, London
Printed and bound in Great Britain by BPC Hazell Books Ltd.
A member of The British Printing Company Ltd.

CONTENTS

ACKNOWLEDGEMENTS

First of all I would like to thank two special heroes of mine, Arthur Oglesby and Hugh Falkus, for the time and trouble they have taken with me in the past. Salmon fishing in this country just would not be the same today without them; and we all owe them an enormous debt for their generosity and involvement. I also consider myself very lucky to have met Richard Waddington recently up in Scotland. Though I did not talk to him deeply, it was a privilege to meet yet another legend and to watch him fish the River Garry so expertly. I would like to thank Borge Munk Jensen, the Danish equivalent of the three gentlemen already mentioned, for his advice on Scandinavian salmon fishing and help with photography.

I would like to recognize Dr Bill Barber for his colossal written contribution on salmon and their life history. Bill is a lovely man, an exceptional scientist and has the happy knack of being able to convey his knowledge in a very easy, accessible fashion. Simon Gawesworth rose to the challenge of describing casting for me ably, generously and quickly. If anglers receive as much from his courses as I did from his letters and phone calls then they will go home very happy men. Dave Steuart is of the same mould, a man who knows his rivers so intimately that it just leaves one amazed. Dave and the Wessex rivers flow together through life, and I thank him for all his help, generosity and fascinating phone conversations.

I met Cecil Thomas in Scotland and was immediately struck by his immense knowledge and warmth. He became a friend in the twinkling of his roguish Welsh eye! Numerous times I have phoned him over the compilation of this book, and at every twist and turn he has delivered exactly the information needed – just like his own Welsh friend, Gordon Heath. Few men know more about fishing and the wild than Gordon, and were it not for the fact that he has to run a very busy hotel, there would not be a fish safe anywhere in the Highlands! Thank you, Gordon, for everything.

Another hotelier of fame is Mike Taylor, proprietor of the Red Lion Hotel in Bredwardine, long famous as a haunt of salmon men. Mike contributed authoritatively to this book and put me in touch with Tony Jones – not the least of his generosities. Tony is a mine of information, which he puts across in a wonderful way that makes you feel in no way ill at ease or belittled. Here is a man that loves salmon, loves fishing and loves teaching. While in Wales, I would also like to thank Peter Smith of the Caer Beris Hotel, Builth Wells, for all his help, encouragement and friendship . . . and the frequent use of his own excellent salmon water!

Richard Johnston is a remarkable young man; he came to stay with me for a few days, caught a couple of big roach, went back to Ireland and then volunteered to write everything he knows about salmon fishing in that beautiful country – which is a very great deal. Thank you very much indeed, Richard, and may your rod always be bent! Another great friend I met in 1993 is Niels Ortoft, a travelling Dane, working in Japan and fishing everywhere. Thank you Niels for all your inspiration, words and photographs. Still on the international scene, I would also like to thank Johan Abelson and Des Elliott for their help with Russia and Ireland respectively. Neither could have been more generous.

Here in Norfolk thanks are due to Jim and

Shirley Deterding, David Clarke, Michael and Audrey Robbins and Richard Gibbs. All of these fine people are far too generous to me, and I know that whenever I phoned for help, advice and encouragement for this book, it was always given. I am eternally grateful for the way that I have plumbed the depths of their coffee, wine, books, experience and hospitality.

Remaining in Norfolk, I would also like the thank Viscount Coke and Mr T. Ronnay at Holkham Hall for allowing me to look through the records and photograph albums there. It was a marvellous experience that I will never forget. Thanks also go to Patrick Veale from Dulverton, who was so quick to respond to my request, and to Terry Weldon, a colleague in the tackle industry, who gave up an afternoon to help me with queries about gear.

I am indebted to Simon Brett, the celebrated angling historian of Gloucestershire for valuable information. A visit to his premises is always something that I look forward to greatly, and I have never been let down. Simon and his wife Edwina are two of the most spirited, knowledgeable and engaging people that one could think of to share an afternoon's salmon talk.

I must also mention and thank Robin Armstrong – excellent artist, angler and friend. May the coming years shine for him!

Finally, I would like to extend my thanks to the ladies. Once again Anne Voss Bark, owner of the excellent Arundell Arms, helped unstintingly and immediately. Thank you, most of all, to the home team for where would I be without Sylvia manning the office side of things and Joy catching all the fish?

Shirley Deterding fishes for salmon around the world from Labrador to the Kola, but here proudly holds a British fish.

1 SALMON AND THE GREAT ANGLERS

A VIEW OF SALMON FISHING

Books need to be justified, especially in these difficult times. This is especially true for fishing books because there are simply so many of them on the market. Any newcomer has to fight to find himself a place on the bookshop shelves. It was easier, of course, many years ago: the earliest books on salmon fishing earned their keep because so little was known about the sport. It was all new ground, and theories could be expressed as fact with little fear of contradiction. Later books flourished because this early knowledge was tested and pushed ever further. The books by Falkus, Oglesby and Waddington and the rest of their colleagues are the great works that I was brought up on, the books that I found under the Christmas tree or unwrapped

I have no hesitation in starting this book with a photograph of Hugh Falkus, a true colossus of the salmon fishing scene.

on birthdays. They are what I read during the winter evenings or at night when I couldn't sleep, worried by exams or life. They guided me in my first steps along the salmon rivers – especially once I'd reached my late teens and had begun to fish more constructively (my childhood fishing, after all, was one long adventure of cuts, bruises, wettings, tangles and very occasional glories).

Then, I counted myself very lucky to have those books. Since, I have been even more fortunate in that I have talked to the three authors mentioned. It is one thing to meet heroes and quite another to find they all measure up to the exalted image one has created for them. Measure up! They tower in knowledge, skill and authority. Obviously, Falkus, Oglesby and Waddington are quite impossible acts to follow, and I am not even going to try. How could I?

I attempt this book because I feel times have changed and that I personify a rather different type of salmon fisherman. I can identify with those beginning, with those who have not caught a thousand fish and with those who do not own a beat or book one for a month at a time during the best of the seasons. My own research amongst tackle shops, hoteliers and magazine editors indicates that a whole new breed of men and women is feeling its way into salmon fishing wherever and whenever there is an opening. This is rather how my own career has been formed.

I know very many older salmon anglers, men who have fished for half a century or more, and I consider them very fortunate indeed. In virtually all cases, their fathers and/or their grandfathers fished. Their families would rent a particular beat, or beats, year upon year, for two, four or even six weeks. The gillies on these beats became like their guardians, friends and mentors, and they grew up with fifteen-foot rods in their hands. This, undoubtedly, is the way to learn. Fishing enters the bloodstream and becomes second nature. You realize this when you watch a man brought up in this way: just the act of casting is almost magical. There is no need to think, hardly even to look, and

still the fly arrows out and lands exactly where it should in the stream. This type of skill is unmatchable. Treasure these sights and these meetings for I'm afraid this breed of salmon angler is on the wane.

The New Breed of Angler

Since the end of the 1940s, two important things have combined to change the face of salmon fishing: beats have become more and more expensive and leisure time has become increasingly scarce. As a result, outside royalty, the high aristocracy and the really big money, it is now very much more difficult to devote the long days to salmon fishing that are required to refine talent into genius. Also, field sports no longer dominate in the way they once did. For example, a twelve-year-old today is more likely to opt for a skiing trip in Austria in March than a fishing trip in Scotland.

However, though we are losing 'career' fishermen, there has been a great increase in the number of casual salmon anglers. I hope this does not sound contradictory. While one group of people has begun to withdraw a little, other sections have rushed in. For instance, many businessmen have begun to find new pleasure in the countryside, in shooting, riding and game fishing. The country hotels that offer clay pigeons, a tacked-up horse or two and fish are today doing very well indeed out of this new class of customers.

There is another important influence at work as well: during the 1960s and 1970s there was a colossal boom in reservoir fly fishing. From the middle of the twentieth century, population increases and the demands of industry and government planning all created a new angling dimension. Vast reservoirs were built to supply the growing populace with water and were stocked with trout. The fish of these waters were as wary as any wild ones and took a great deal of catching. Chew, Grafham and Rutland soon attracted thousands of anglers away from coarse fishing and onto the fly. A sound angling background allowed men like Bob Church,

Cyril Inwood and T.C. Ivens soon to become experts. Countless anglers followed in their footsteps and considered themselves game anglers. These men had holidays as well and in them began to look for something else, something wilder and something more challenging: a great many found this in annual weeks spent fly fishing. These soon became the highlight of their angling years.

These two groups of anglers more than made up for the slight decline in the traditional class of salmon fishermen, and this is certainly true today. Far more salmon anglers are pursuing far fewer fish. The pressure on rivers, has, therefore, increased, and the price of salmon fishing, in most cases, has risen. Indeed, several of the people who helped me with this book expressed grave reservations, especially when I said that the purpose of the work is to inspire as much as to teach and to recruit as many new fishermen as possible to the ranks. 'Do we want

salmon fishing highlighted?' they asked. 'Do we need more men and women competing for beats?' 'Aren't rivers bursting as they are?' Certainly I sympathize with this few, but surely salmon are best safeguarded by swelling the numbers of those who support them. The more people who are personally involved with salmon, the more people there will be to pressure governments to stop netting at sea, to hammer polluters and poachers and to temper barrage schemes that will interfere with the runs of migratory fish. Salmon are still very much at risk and need all the friends they can get, especially those with a modern environmentally progressive attitude.

Thus, I hope I can justify this book: I am trying to speak to the amateur salmon fisher, to encourage him, and to make him believe that the salmon is not a deified species beyond his ability.

I certainly needed help writing this book. My

Dusk creeps along Hugh Falkus' home river.

own salmon career is patchy – typical perhaps of many younger anglers in the sport – not particularly blessed with background or opportunity. I was lucky in that my parents were sympathetic and sent me on several salmon holidays from the age of ten or thereabouts to north Wales, north Lancashire and the Hampshire Avon. As a result, I had landed thirty or so fish by the time I was taking my 'O' Levels. Since then I have attempted to catch salmon on eighteen rivers throughout the UK and have added around another three hundred fish to my earlier tallies. Perhaps more importantly, I have found nearly as many friends as I have caught salmon, and many of them have helped unstintingly with this book.

I began writing in 1993, the 400th anniversary of Izaak Walton's birth. Walton, you might know, talked a great deal about the brotherhood of the angle. He actually enlisted the help of the aristocrat Charles Cotton to contribute the game fishing section to a later edition of *The Compleat Angler*. Walton had many very good friends and even had rooms reserved for him all around the country so that he could follow his sport wherever and whenever he wished. It was rather nice for me to see that the same type of attitude exists today, and I have been able to call on the help of friends from Japan to Devon, from Connemara to Invernessshire, from Norway to Hampshire.

If salmon have long been a part of my life, then the last six months it has been immersed in them and the people who fish for them. I can now understand just why salmon are so special and such a symbol of nature at its most precious. There was one moment in Devon, in August 1993, when I got up early and walked two miles upstream to begin fishing just as the light crept into the heavily wooded valley around me. This was a mysterious, almost primeval place, and I could hear my heart beating loudly – or was it just the footsteps of elves round me in the forest. Don't laugh: fishermen know that distinctions between past and present can be dissolved, and that reality and fantasy can merge.

Anyway, I hooked a salmon as the sun rose. It ran, and then it leapt in very shallow water and threw droplets everywhere. Then it came free. For a while the ripples washed against the rocks of the pool, and then everything was still. You can easily imagine the beauty, the drama and the utter privilege I felt in being a witness to the scene. I offer it as just a glimpse of why salmon must be cherished and why so many anglers must get involved in the fight to preserve them. If salmon should ever dwindle and die, what an indictment that would be of us all. It would be the final admission of failure, the final proof that our society is bankrupt and we have nothing but emptiness to pass on to those that follow.

NOTES ON THE ATLANTIC SALMON

Dr Bill Barber has been a fish biologist for quarter of a century or more and for ten years has run his own fish farm on Loch Lochy in Invernessshire. There are, therefore, few people better equipped to discuss the life of the salmon, the problems that it faces and the dangers threatening its environment today.

In the kingdom of the fish there are some extraordinary performers. There is much intricate behaviour such as nest building, pair bonding and aggression, amazing camouflage techniques, air-breathing, talking and even more sex changing than in the average Sunday tabloid. Less common are fish that walk over land, generate considerable electric charges and live lives as parasitic males permanently fused to the larger bulk of a female. The feeding habits of fish are equally varied: giants filter-feed on crustacea, and small deep-sea gulpers swallow prey as big as themselves. There are many fishy vegetarians that feed on algae or larger plants, while the great white shark feeds on – well, whatever it wants! Consider, finally, their range – from the deepest, widest ocean to the highest torrential mountain streams. There are even fish living in tem-

Fishery research began in the nineteenth century.

porary water that regularly dries up. They either have short sharp lives and resistant eggs, or they burrow into the mud and curl up in a damp cocoon of congealed mucus to survive!

In Britain there are two species that do their best to span this range, swimming thousands of miles from adult feeding waters to spawn. These fish – eels and salmon – are contrasting in appearance. Whilst some aspects of the eels' migration out to breed in the Atlantic Sargasso Sea remain a mystery, the determined upstream and even overland migration of the young elvers is a source of amazement. The salmon, arriving in rivers sleek and silvery from the sea to battle upstream, fasting and changing appearance before they finally spawn on the gravels that were once their own nurseries, strike a nobler pose, embodying many of the elements of romanticism. No wonder the salmon is known widely as the King of Fish.

Spawning

Spawning adult salmon return to fresh water after spending one or more years at sea. They can enter fresh water any time from spring until early autumn. Generally, grilse (fish that have spent only one year at sea and weigh two to three kilograms) swim through the estuary and lower sluggish reaches to where the river flows faster with a bed of rocks and gravels. They arrive later than bigger salmon. The fish lie up in pools and gradually make their way to the spawning grounds. These are typically shallow gravels where the current is always sufficient to keep the beds clean of silt that might otherwise smother the eggs and the delicate gills of newly hatched alevins.

By the time they reach their spawning grounds, they have changed from the sleek silvery fish that first ran the gauntlet of seals, netsmen, anglers and poachers. The females become heavy with eggs and darker in colour,

This is a quite different fish. It is a slim grilse of only five or six pounds that has probably spent a year at sea.

A mighty River Wye springer – all forty-plus pounds of it.

while the males develop a hooked and pro-truding lower jaw, commonly called a kype. On the gravels, the females cut short trenches or redds, and the males vie with one another to fertilize the eggs as they are shed into these redds. Among this heaving and swirling mass of two- to ten-kilogram fish, tiny precocious male parr can also be found shedding viable sperm. The biological significance of this phenomenon is not fully understood, but it could enable fertilization to be maximized in situations where adult males are outnumbered by the females.

After spawning, the adults are a sad sight, having converted most of their fat and oil reserves into eggs, sperm and energy. Even their muscle tissue has been wasted to enable

the fish to achieve the ultimate goal of spawn-ing. Their skin, already in physiological stress from coping with the change from sea water to fresh water, has often been physically dam-aged by the efforts of migrating upstream and the process of spawning itself. In shallow water, it is believed that ultraviolet light further damages the delicate single-cell epider-mis that covers the fish's body (including the scales) and maintains its important, protective slime. Spawned-out salmon (kelts) are prone to rapid infection by fungus and bacteria, and many (especially the males) soon die. Depend-ing upon circumstances, such as temperature, the nature of the river and water level, the fish can nevertheless survive, run out to sea and return a year or so later, once again sleek silver salmon intent on their near-suicidal mission to reproduce.

It has been argued that by dying after spawning, the adults' ultimate sacrifice increases the chances of survival for their young by fertilizing with their bodies an otherwise impoverished environment. It is, perhaps, more likely that death is the inevitable consequence of putting so much effort into a system of spawning that involves so many stresses, like moving from marine to fresh water, spending up to six months without feeding, turning up to ten per cent of body weight into gonads and battling up sometimes torrential rivers and streams to cut redds or compete with other fish to spawn successfully.

In situations where there is an overabundance of returning adults or – perhaps more likely these days – a reduction in the area of spawning grounds because of low water levels, silting or access difficulties, late-arriving fish can destroy the redds of early spawners. During spawning some eggs are always washed downstream, where they are greatly appreciated by various animals, from scavenging invertebrates to birds and fishes. Many more eggs will be lost if redds are overcut, and this may well be a self-regulation mechanism, designed to reduce the chances of overpopulating the river with fry.

The Young Fish

Once fertilized and lodged between the gravels of the spawning grounds, the eggs are relatively safe. Development is temperature-related and therefore slow, since ambient temperatures range between two and five degrees Centigrade. At the southern end of their range, salmon eggs might hatch within two months, but further north it could take twice as long. Thus, in March or April the typical salmon egg will hatch, and a fry with a hugely swollen belly will appear. This swelling is the egg sac, and the fish is called the alevin. Alevins remain relatively inactive in the gravels for a further month or so, gradually absorbing the yoke reserves in the sac and developing into fully functioning little fish.

Eventually, small fish weighing next to nothing emerge from the gravels and start the long and dangerous business of growing up. Salmon fry – called parr once they develop characteristic parr marks – are territorial and spread out through the river system. By migrating to the headwaters of rivers to spawn, salmon ensure that their offspring can utilize as much of the river system as possible, as it is easier for them to drift downstream to find suitable territories than to struggle up. A suitable territory is a spot where the fish can lie up out of the main current and not so much actively forage for food within this territory but intercept suitable items drifting past.

There is competition for territories not just among the siblings of one redd and contemporaries from others, but to some extent from the older parr of the previous year's spawning activities. Young fry are vulnerable, unaware of the dangers around them, least able to dart to safety and of a size that can allow them to fall victim to large invertebrates, such as the fully grown nymphs of carnivorous stone flies. Even if larger, older parr do not represent a major threat by competing for food (because they will tend to feed on larger food items), they may still aggressively defend their territories against the young parr. The longer these baby parr spend unsettled, the greater their vulnerability to predation.

Different burns, becks, streams and rivers will all have different potentials for fish production, based upon temperature, water chemistry (which determines the potential of plant growth) and the physical nature of the stream (whether it is a torrential spating burn or a steady gentle stream with pools and ripples and the amount and types of biological material which is carried into the water).

In upland streams (typical salmon parr habitat) much of the invertebrate life and therefore parr food consists of plants and animal material falling into the river. Terrestrial insects can form a significant part of the salmon parr's diet, while leaf litter is important food for lots of aquatic invertebrates such as mayflies, stone flies and caddis flies, which are themselves important as food for fish. Therefore, the nature of the plants lining the river banks is all important: native hardwood trees and herbaceous plants will generally provide a rich larder of terrestrial insects and useful leaf litter. Banks of rhododendrons, perhaps attractive to us in June, are relatively sterile, as is the leaf litter of conifer plantations, which can have a harmful acidifying effect on run-off water.

Smolts and Grilse

Parr take a variable time to become smolts, typically between two and four years. This allows the system to become more flexible, and a salmon population can recover from a disastrous spawning year. If spawning is particularly poor one year, then the next year's fry will experience less competition for territory and food, and some may smolt a year early.

There are other implications of the territorial nature of salmon parr. Put crudely, a stretch of river has a finite capacity to produce smolts, for example one thousand fifty-gram smolts each year. Some years it might produce two thousand twenty-five gram smolts. This, however, will not necessarily mean more returning adult salmon since there is a correlation between the percentage returns (that is the number of smolts leaving and the number of adults returning) and smolt size and vigour.

It is quite possible that the common practice of 'topping-up' streams and burns with eyed eggs and young parr is anything from pointless to detrimental – pointless because the newly introduced parr will not find any worthwhile territories in an already stocked system, detrimental because more does not always mean better. One hundred thousand poor smolts may achieve only one per cent return and therefore one thousand returning adults. Fifty thousand large and healthy smolts may have a ten per cent survival and generate five thousand returning adults. When measured,

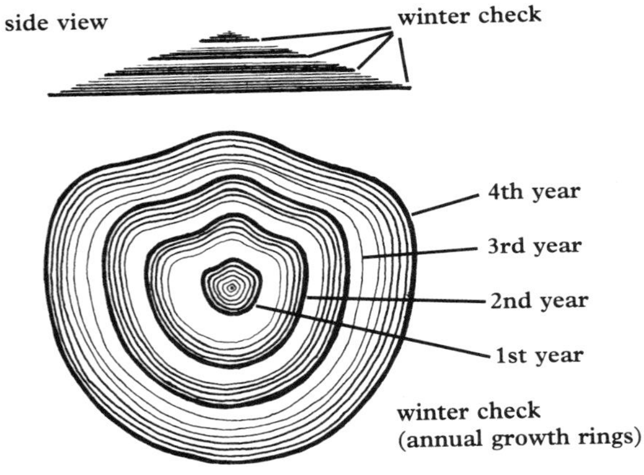

side view · winter check
4th year
3rd year
2nd year
1st year
winter check
(annual growth rings)

A salmon scale consists of a pile of plates.

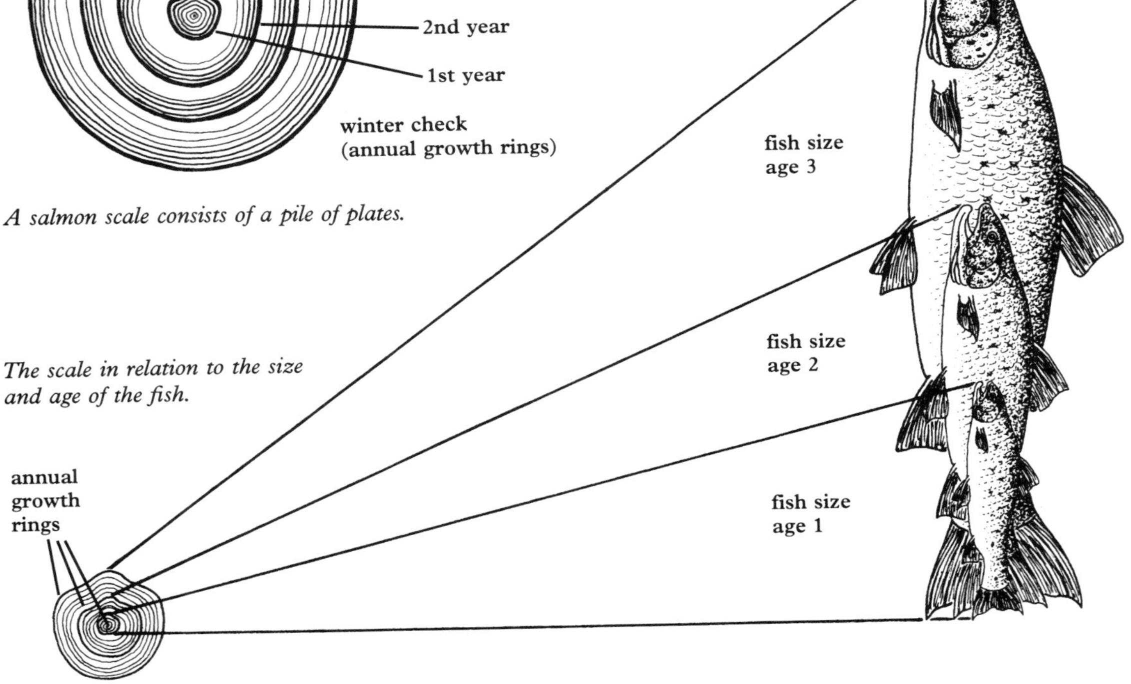

The scale in relation to the size and age of the fish.

annual growth rings

fish size age 3

fish size age 2

fish size age 1

returns vary between one per cent and rare highs of twenty per cent. This is perhaps why the salmon themselves sometimes apparently wastefully overcut their redds. It could be a method to help prevent an initial overstocking of parr from a particularly strong year class of returning adults. In theory, sufficient over-stocking, if combined with high parr survival rates, could lead to such poor parr growth that for a year or so, no fish would grow big enough to become smolts.

Given enough time and food, the parr will grow to between twenty-five and fifty grams or so in the spring and begin to smolt. Losing their parr marks, they take on the appearance of small silvery salmon, and they prepare for their journey downstream and out to sea and the challenge of moving from fresh to salt water. Changes take place in their skin, and enzyme levels change in their blood to enable them to cope with the physical and physiologi-cal traumas that lie ahead.

The fish must negotiate all the hazards that their parents encountered years earlier but at least they are going downstream. They are disadvantaged by their small size, barely one per cent of that of their parents, and are still vulnerable to many predators. Given sufficient water, the falls that their parents leapt are no danger. Man-made obstacles can be more sig-nificant. Hydro-turbines can be especially fatal. Whilst some rivers flow quickly out to sea, some smolts must negotiate the more pol-luted lower reaches of other rivers. At sea, they have the advantages of new and usually abundant food sources, but dangers from new predators exist. Cormorants, seals and other big fish replace the otters, pike, goosanders and herons of fresh water.

The fish that are to spend several years at sea head north and then north-west to feed and then to grow fat on the same kind of food that supports blue whales off the south of Greenland. When these feeding grounds were discovered by commercial fishermen some years ago, the last safe refuge of the Atlantic salmon had disappeared.

Eventually, after one year as so-called grilse or two or more years as larger salmon, the fish head back to the rivers of their birth. It is believed they navigate initially by magnetism and then by smell. They then run the same gauntlet as their parents did two to seven years earlier. They return, not to their genetic home, but up the river they came out of as smolts. Thus, fish transferred as egg fry or smolts to a new river system will return to the new system.

Salmon under Threat

Like other living things salmon require a special place to live (a habitat) that provides them with all of their needs. As a migratory animal, the salmon has a range of habitat requirements for the different stages in its life-cycle. Unlike migratory birds, salmon cannot bypass an unsuitable zone or barrier created by man's latest activity. To survive in a river system there must be accessible areas of clean gravels for spawning and incubation, places for parr to grow on, safe passage for smolts to the sea, safe migratory routes and fishing grounds for the fish at sea and finally safe access for the returning mature fish to carry on the cycle. Their life follows a long chain through a range of habitats, and with just one missing link the salmon will disappear from an entire system.

All these stages are fraught with natural dangers: spates and floods threaten young fish and eggs, while salmon are always vulnerable to a range of predators. Natural physical bar-riers pose problems for the migrating adults and smolts, and lack of fresh water can be as significant a hazard as too much, denying adult access to headwaters and even leaving eggs and fry stranded or vulnerable to frost.

Since man extended his range and his 'abili-ties', the salmon's problems have been com-pounded. Initially, man's impact was limited to harvesting the vulnerable returning adults, but with the development of communities all man's activities have proved harmful to salmon. Freshwater habitats reflect the activi-ties of the surrounding land, and man quickly developed techniques that caused degra-dation. Soon water was used for irrigation sys-tems, waste disposal transport, power and drainage control. All these activities have proved detrimental to the ecology of the water by direct pollution or by changes in flow pat-terns, by increasing silt or by creating physical barriers that the migrating fish have to overcome.

It is worth repeating that salmon have to overcome many problems in their complicated and demanding pattern of life. A few miles of deoxygenated water at the lower reach of a river can be devastating to the whole salmon population of the system since twice in its life-cycle it has to try to swim through it. An innocuous but poorly designed turbine can have a dramatic effect on a river if typical rainfall patterns mean that the weir system deflects all the migrating smolts through the turbine. Agricultural and forestry practices can change the nature of a river, gradually degrading its ability to sustain salmon. Clear felling can increase erosion so that spawning grounds become silted. Acidification will also cause decreases in productivity.

The Impact of Salmon Farming

There is yet another threat to the salmon's survival, and this concerns the consequences of its direct exploitation by man. Salmon are exploited in three main ways: by commercial fishing, by angling and – more recently – as a subject for fish farming. In the last decade or so the development of salmon farming, often in close proximity to wild populations, has caused considerable concern. In the UK the process involves a freshwater stage – first in hatcheries then in tanks or freshwater cages – followed by a sea stage, when the smolts are transferred to cages at sites where sea-lochs and islands provide some shelter.

There is concern that large intensive salmon farms spread disease to wild populations and that escapes of juveniles from fresh water or adult fish from sea cages could have additional effects on wild populations. Finally, the dis-charges from big farms can have the same potentially harmful effects as any other dis-charge into an aquatic environment.

While intensive aquaculture, like any other kind of farming, creates husbandry problems, and salmon farmers have experienced dilemmas with diseases, there has been no evi-dence of these spreading to wild populations. Perhaps we should be more worried by the threat farming poses to the genetic nature of wild salmon.

Salmon running into different river systems tend to show different patterns of behaviour. For example, some run early and some run late. There are also differences in their appear-ance: some fish are very much shorter and deeper than others. Commercial farmers have exploited these differences, developing strains by crossing stock from different rivers, (even countries) to develop characteristics best suited for culture. Recent studies have con-firmed that these differences are indeed gen-etic. There is a distinct possibility that escapees could thus dilute the natural gene pool (the range of genes naturally found in a population responsible for the natural vari-ation within that population) of a wild popu-lation. With salmon farming concentrating on growing on a few preferred strains, it is possi-ble that the limited gene pool of these developed strains could come to dominate the genetic variety in wild populations if escapees start to dominate.

It is considered that the bigger the gene pool populations have, the better they are at adapting to or resisting change. For example, a healthy population with a big gene pool may be confronted with a new disease. While many fish may be vulnerable, with a wide variety in the population, some other fish may be resist-ant and thus survive to pass on their resistance to the next generation.

In a similar way, variations between popu-lations in different river systems not only enable the populations to utilize, or cope with, subtle differences in the systems, they also give the species as a whole a greater ability to adapt to change as it comes. Any reduction in gen-etic variety because of mass escapes of farm strains could thus be a significant threat to the health of wild salmon populations in the future. Mass escapes of adults or juveniles could also have an impact on the general ecol-ogy of a stream, river or even sea-loch.

On a positive side, the reduction in the price of salmon flesh caused by farming has taken some pressure off wild stocks by undermining the viability of some commercial fish oper-ations. Also, the improvement in husbandry techniques made by commercial farming can be applied to the propagation of wild fish, to help reinstate or maintain wild populations.

Salmon are threatened by direct harvesting as the subject of commercial and sport fisheries. While angling is confined to fresh water, and anglers and fishery owners tend to appreciate that sufficient salmon must be allowed to reach their spawning grounds, commercial fishing is rarely conscious of conversation. Salmon are taken by a variety of methods – not all of which are legal. While their reduction in numbers and high value in the sport fisheries has led to an increasing trend towards buying up and closing down commercial fisheries, the very nature of salmon and their predictable migration times and routes will always make them vulnerable, and their value will always make any effort or risk worthwhile.

Valuing the Salmon
Finally, I would like to propose a basic and somewhat crude model in order to discuss some of the implications of survival rates, population manipulation and the economic value of salmon. The model is based on the following reasonable assumptions: one hundred fish survive to spawn each year (half male and half female), females produce eight thousand eggs for every kilo of their total body weight, there is a ten per cent return to the fishery as two-and-a-half-kilogram grilse and there is an eighty per cent harvest by the fishery. The following calculations can now be made.

Number of eggs laid	
2½ × 50 × 8000	1,000,000
Total number of adults returning	500
Number of smolts produced	5,000
Number of adults harvested	400
Total weight of salmon harvested	1,000kg

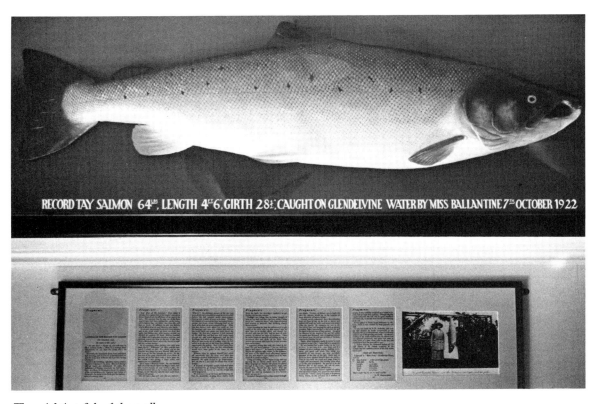

RECORD TAY SALMON 64ᴸᴮ, LENGTH 4ᶠᵀ6, GIRTH 28½, CAUGHT ON GLENDELVINE WATER BY MISS BALLANTINE 7ᵀᴴ OCTOBER 1922

The mightiest fish of them all.

The model shows a high mortality rate from egg to adult (inevitable if rivers are not to become blocked with returning adults) and even from egg to smolt. The value of the fishery obviously depends upon the value given to the fish taken. As a commercial fishery, a price of £5 per kilogram would give a total value of £5,000. As a sport fishery, the value of salmon has been estimated as high as £800 per fish (to the whole community for fish caught in the River Wye). Such a figure would value the fishery at £320,000.

The high value of salmon returning to a sport fishery not only justifies arguments about protecting them from commercial fisheries but also the cost of fish enhancement programmes. As long ago as 1974, various agencies along the Columbia River in the USA spent $10 million releasing 140 million smolts into the system. The fishery is estimated to be worth $75 million a year, and half the fish caught have a hatchery origin.

Imagine that one wishes to spend £100 on improving fish stocks. The money could be spent on ten thousand eggs at £10 per thousand or a hundred smolts at £1 each. Even if one assumed (or knew) that the system could cope with more eggs and produce a corresponding number of smolts, the mortality rate predicted by the model (egg to smolt) means that ten thousand eggs will produce only fifty smolts. Thus, stocking with eggs is not necessarily the most cost effective way to increase the number of smolts leaving a system.

It is interesting to note that at a smolt cost of £1 each and a value of returning salmon of £100, it is only when return rates fall to one per cent that the releasing of smolts to enhance a fishery ceases to show a positive cost benefit.

With returning adults producing eight thousand eggs per kilogram, one successful pair of breeding salmon can produce a lot of eggs. If smolts are not available for an enhancement programme, efforts may be best spent in improving and maintaining access for spawning adults, minimizing dangers for migrating smolts and trying to improve the nature of the streams and rivers in the system to maximize the natural production of smolts.

I hope I have given you some insight into the demanding and vulnerable nature of salmon – demanding because they require a series of natural unspoilt habitats to survive, vulnerable because these habitats are under considerable threat and the fish themselves are being hunted. It is not surprising to see their ranges declining. In part it is natural. Since the last Ice Age, the seas have warmed and the southern limit of their natural range has shifted north. However, more dramatic has been the impact of man's activities.

The general increase in environmental awareness may well help safeguard the habitats essential for the salmon's survival into the next century, but a growing realization of the real economic value of angling may be the eventual salvation of the salmon. It is now reasonable to argue that wild salmon are too valuable to be a commercial species. The only thing certain is that every effort must continue if we wish to have the chance to catch or even to see salmon leaping up British waters in the next century.

UNDERSTANDING SALMON

I suppose I'd better be careful right from the start and say that the title of this chapter itself is a very dubious one. It is fashionable to say that fish are creatures that one can never actually understand fully and that they will always spring surprises. This much is quite true. At the same time, I don't think it is fair to say that the salmon or any other fish is a complete mystery to us. So many observant anglers and scientists have watched salmon and other fish for so many centuries that we do have more than a clue about what is going on.

For most salmon anglers over the centuries probably the leading topic of conversation has been why the species does not feed upon its return to fresh water to spawn and yet takes worms, prawns, spinners and flies, often with great eagerness.

For those serious about wanting to know, Hugh Falkus' great book *Salmon* has many of the clues, especially the excellent, if not epic, chapter on taking behaviour. Mr Falkus uses the apt phrase 'variable reluctance' when he comes to describe the salmon's desire to open its mouth. Another source of information that must be read and understood if you really want to know the fish you are after is Professor Peter Behan's contribution to *Salmon and Women – The Feminine Angle*.

I live in a very pleasant country estate, which has two large lakes in its grounds, connected by a narrow winding reed-fringed canal. Recently I acquired a canoe, which is a magical tool for allowing me to glide round on summer evenings and observe the fish in the lakes. One of the most interesting discoveries for me was that pike appeared to feed in either of the two lakes and then retire to the canal to digest their prey. Day after day the same pike would be seen in the same positions absolutely comatose. It was almost possible to lift them out of the water with the oar. After there had been a wind strong enough to stir the water to some degree, these pikes were also virtually covered with silt so that they looked like sunken logs but for their eyes. What I am trying to say here is that obviously several fish species will ignore food totally until something triggers them into action.

What Makes a Salmon Feed?

To go back to salmon, I believe that there are conditions that make them very, very positive in their behaviour – vibrant even – alert and alive enough to have a snap at anything that resembles their foodstuffs of the past. We have all seen it. One day salmon are sulking moodily at the bottom of pools, and the next they are finning the water – quivering bars of silver, moving backwards and forwards, leaping, pushing up moving water fast – quite obviously with a mind to get things done. It is at these times that the fly or lure is likely to be taken. What the angler must establish, then, is when these prime times occur.

Here I must mention another book, *Salmon Taking Times*, written by Reg Righyni in 1965.

For anybody wanting to understand the salmon, this is an excellent book that shows a desire to search into the ill-understood corners of the salmon fishing world. For example, Righyni wanted to test out that supposed sixth sense possessed by some salmon fishermen and look into why and when salmon do in fact take. What Righyni produced was an unusually keen look at the water and a searching examination of river life.

One of the two principal themes of the book is the salmon's need for oxygen. This is isolated as the only external factor at work on salmon in a British river. Righyni looks at the availability and the accessibility of oxygen to the salmon and reasons that a specific level of availability of oxygen for the fish produces a surge of energy. The fish reaches a climax of mental and physical activity when oxygen availability is at its peak, and it is then that a fly stands the greatest chance of being taken. Righyni goes on to anticipate taking times by looking at weather and water factors and ends by forecasting the possible taking times on any river in any given situation.

In my opinion, this concept is central: something makes salmon switch on. Something produces this surge of interest in the world around them. It is typical of Righyni to understand this, for the book presents one of the clearest understandings of water as an element ever produced by a fisherman. Righyni had the reputation as the best grayling fisherman in Yorkshire and was able to control and watch a float at over eighty yards. Who could be more capable of investigating the laws of water and why the salmon must obey them? His feel for the water was born of observation, love and intuition. Describing the body of a salmon river, he becomes a bankside scientist ready to isolate and analyse the very last oxygen bubble. What Professor Behan does with clinical efficiency, Righyni does with passion and practical experience.

I personally find the oxygen theory very convincing indeed. It is much more usual to read that water temperature is the key to triggering

Testing the waters. Temperature is all-important.

the fish into activity. Most books, therefore, tend to give temperature ranges at which the fish are most likely to take the fly. Bitingly cold water usually gets the thumbs-down as does warm water – the latter especially as the salmon is primarily a cold-water fish and is restricted to the northern latitudes. Only a fool would deny that temperature and the changing of a river as spring develops into summer do not have an influence on salmon behaviour and their willingness to take the fly.

Salmon Senses

Anybody who wants to catch a salmon would do well not to underestimate the highly developed senses of this fish. It is primarily a creature that hunts visually and its eyesight is extraordinarily good. If you approach a river carelessly, and you see a salmon that doesn't move, that is almost certainly because it does not care to, not because it has not seen you. It is the same with hearing and the ability to pick up vibration. Quite simply, the angler who approaches each pool with caution, wades very carefully and as quietly as possible, tries to avoid being seen against sky lines and uses every scrap of cover wherever he can will catch more fish – other things being equal of course. The best tackle and techniques will be absolutely useless if the fish have been scared out of the pool in the first place. This attention to approach is obviously all the more important, the shallower, clearer and smaller the river is.

We finish, for the moment, on scent – a major reason, Professor Behan argues, for women catching more salmon than men. The idea is that the salmon's sense of smell is extraordi-

My father's cigarette box, now converted to flies. Did the odour of nicotine put fish off until it wore away?

I don't know whether what follows should be seen as a cautionary tale or simply coincidence. When my father died, I converted his silver cigarette box to a holder for my salmon flies. The idea was to keep in touch with him during the most pleasing times of my life and to use a very attractive article in a positive way. My father died in 1977, and I began using the cigarette box in the spring of that year. Believe it or not, flies from the box proved very unsuccessful for several years. I do not say I never caught salmon on flies from the box because that would not be true, but they did seem less successful than others from elsewhere. Looking back, I wonder whether the smell of nicotine that must have lingered around the box could in some way have tainted the flies I was using for a number of years until repeated trips to the great outdoors somehow purged them. Certainly, I will never dream of taking liberties with salmon sensibilities again.

SALMON LIES AND POOLS

Never be ashamed of admitting that you do not read a new river correctly at the very first meeting. Trout and salmon differ vastly, and while it is very possible to go to a new stretch of water and gauge almost exactly where the best of the trout lies will be, the same cannot be said for salmon. This is a very different species altogether. I suppose one of the major reasons for gillies playing such an important role in salmon fishing and not in trout fishing is that the local man will know exactly where the fish are.

I know two stretches of salmon river very well. One is on the upper Garry and the other is on the middle Wye – waters as different from each other as you can imagine. On the upper Garry I have just an inkling now, after thirty or forty trips, where fish might be lying in certain water conditions, but I am never sure and a fish hooked never mind landed is always something of an achievement. Mind you, there is a man in the glen who seems to know the most

narily highly developed, and fish can detect the minute chemical differences given off by men and women – the former unpleasant or frightening, the latter not so unpleasant or even attractive in some way. I simply do not know about this. After all, the dace that caught the record salmon for Miss Ballantine was actually hooked on by her father, so presumably it was tainted by a male rather than female scent. In any case, the important point to consider is that salmon can detect odours in the water, and therefore it makes sense to treat every bait, lure or fly very carefully indeed.

obscure lies that are never fished and always seem to produce salmon for him in the most unpromising of conditions. Of course, he was catching salmon from the upper Garry years and years before I had even seen the place, and it shows over and over again.

Exactly the same situation holds on the middle Wye, this big, deep rolling river where there are few clues to where the salmon will hold up. However, trip after trip I have seen salmon move at the same place without a single logical explanation. There is, for example, one long featureless glide where salmon jump in exactly the same place, night after night throughout the season. What is it in that unprepossessing stretch of water that seems to attract them? Even in very low water, when I have been able to wade out and investigate, there has been nothing to give me anything like a sensible clue.

Both these examples show, I believe, why gillies to the newcomer or even the experienced fishermen are so essential. Certainly, the gillies on the Wye seem to know where a salmon will

jump five minutes before it actually does so! It also helps explain why salmon fishermen are often very happy to rent the same beat year after year. This does not represent caution or conservatism but the fact that to get to know a stretch of river you really have to visit it as often as possible.

Pools

I am sorry if this is beginning to sound rather defeatist, and I will try to be more optimistic, admitting that there are landmarks on the salmon river that you can look out for. Everybody, for example, has heard of a salmon pool; the trouble is explaining exactly what a 'pool' is. On some rivers this is very easy, and it simply describes an area of deep, fishable water where salmon tend to congregate in numbers on their way upstream. On some of the larger rivers these pools can be quite substantial, but on a river like the Barle they may be absolutely tiny. None the less, they will always attract fish if the conditions are right. On some other rivers

A huge salmon-holding pool on the Tummel. Something this size is probably best fished by boat.

A massive pool, three hundred yards long. Salmon can be found anywhere along its length. The locals, however, know the perfect taking spots.

(I remember being shown a pool on the Tummel), pools can be absolutely immense – hundreds of yards long – and knowing exactly where the fish will be lying is a task in itself, which calls for either great experience or the services of a gillie. However, most salmon beats do have named pools, and these should be the starting point for anybody new to the river.

Whenever I am shown a new pool, I like to look at it carefully for a long time, often without a rod. It is all too easy to be overcome with excitement and start thrashing the water without paying any real attention to the river itself. In fact, if at all possible, I like to arrive at the river a day before fishing and walk the beat, thinking out some sort of strategy. If I have somebody who knows the river with me at the time, then I am even happier with this approach.

Many pools have especially deep runs, and salmon will generally be found in these areas when the river is very cold, very dirty and really boiling through. They will also be found in these deep runs when the water is very shallow, very clear and very warm. These are the two extremes, and outside them salmon seem to prefer shallower more exciting pieces of river.

Of course, when a river is really pounding through, fishing is very difficult indeed, and salmon can be almost anywhere. I always start looking for them very close in under the banks when this happens, partly because tackle is much easier to control in these circumstances if you do not have a great deal of line out. One thing that fishing in a flood does teach you, I think, is the importance of snags to salmon.

Salmon like to lie around some obstruction or obstacle in the river. Of this there can be no doubt. That obstruction can be anything from a boulder to a fallen tree to – on the Wye at least – the long cleaned skeleton of an unfortunate cow! The interesting thing is exactly where the salmon will lie in relation to the obstruction. It is not usual to find the fish tucked in

Salmon will often lie the day out, especially under the branches of low-slung trees.

right behind the snag, where you might expect to find it. It is more likely to take up position in front of, by the side of, or above the obstruction, and these areas are the ones to fish hard.

I suppose my own favourite salmon lies – the areas that I have taken most of my salmon from over the years – have been towards the tails of pools or even lochs. I was told many years ago on the River Lune that salmon frequently rest at the tails of pools after struggling up the white-water into them. I don't know whether that is how the salmon thinks exactly, but I have certainly done very well by concentrating on those last few yards of shallowing water. It could well be that this early advice instilled in

me some confidence on this type of water, and I simply perform that little bit better.

The same type of attraction lies in loch fishing. Let me give the example of Poulary, a hundred-acre loch on the Garry system. Salmon are taken here and there throughout the whole water of the loch, but the real killing area is the point where it empties out through a cascade of falls into the Garry River. The trick is to take a boat out into the loch, anchor it at a 150 yards above the falls and then fish down, letting your boat drop a few yards every five minutes or so. There is great excitement in this fishing, for every so often a big fish will be hooked, turn tail and go down the fast water where you cannot follow. Once I beached myself and managed to keep pace, running along the bank through the heather, but I still lost it. There is also the uneasy feeling that as the current speeds up, the boat could get caught and you might be washed away into the white-water. It hasn't happened, and it probably never will, but it adds a certain edge to the fishing.

Currents

Current speed is important to the salmon. I think they like a good push of water around them but close to slack areas where they can drift if they wish. As I write, I have in mind a stretch of the River Inver. In the summer the salmon lie along a shallow pool where the water ripples about two to three feet deep. The push of the water is consistent and obviously reassuring, for fish are always there nosing it, letting it work along them, occasionally flashing as they roll to let it caress them.

What salmon obviously do not like is a complete absence of current – the sort of condition that prevails frequently in the summer on stretches of the Wye, for example. Without rain, the big river just slows down and comes almost to a complete standstill. The salmon act as though they are marooned in the doldrums, fretting to feel water moving on their faces again and be off upstream. You have to feel sorry for the big fish, turning increasingly red, flopping around hopelessly in these pools of stagnant Wye.

Talking of the Wye, this is a good time to mention the name Robert Pashley. There can be little doubt that in catching terms, Pashley was the most successful British salmon fisherman of all time. This was to an extent because he spent so much time on the river and that in turn led to his complete understanding of this difficult water. In fact, he knew it so well that he frequently turned down invitations to fish water because he knew that other beats would be performing better on the same day.

This was unerring knowledge, built up over decades of experience, and though Pashley could fish a bit too, it was his complete knowledge of where the fish would be lying and taking on any particular day that reaped him such fantastic rewards. There will never be another fisherman like Pashley, for there is neither the time nor the salmon stock left. The lesson, however, remains: learn as much about your river as you possibly can, and bit by bit that fascinating jigsaw of the salmon lie will begin to take shape in your mind. Then you will reap the full reward.

OTHER SALMON OF THE WORLD

Pacific Salmon

It is only fair to have a look at other salmon species available. Probably none is quite as emotive as the Atlantic, but each is a very fine fish in its own right. I suppose pride of place must go to the king salmon of the Pacific Ocean, often called the chinook after the tribe which believed the fish was a supernatural being that ascended the streams for man's use, died and – after the natives returned the bones back to the sea – resumed its original form only to return the following year.

The very size of the king salmon encourages myth and fantasy. This is truly a huge member of the salmon family, and kings have been caught to over ninety pounds on rod and line. A 126-pounder was caught in a fish trap in Alaska just after the Second World War. Apparently the tail span of this fish alone was seventeen and a half inches! The average size is around thirty pounds and fifty-pounders are quite common, so it is hardly surprising that they have a large and devoted following. Alaska appears to be one of the best places to contact kings, and most techniques seem to revolve around using fresh herrings or large spinners and spoons. Fishing windows are quite restricted as runs of king salmon are fairly short in duration, and the first migration in much of

Alaska takes place from mid-May through June with runs petering out at the end of the latter. A second run takes place later on in July with more very big fish ascending the river.

Lucky Pacific anglers often rate the silver salmon as an even greater prize than the king. Silvers are also known as cohos and are the second-largest of the five species of these Pacific fish. Silver salmon are extremely handsome, with a streamlined shape and small scales that glisten. Their weight averages around ten pounds, although on the Kodiak River the average is probably nearer fifteen. A twenty-five pounder is exceptionally large. However, it is not size that attracts anglers to fishing the silvers. Apparently, their fighting ability is absolutely second to none, and a fifteen-pound silver taken on the fly will provide a battle that no angler will ever be able to forget.

The next Pacific salmon on the list is the sockeye. It has a strange name, which comes from the original Indian word *saukie*, which means 'the chief of fishes'. Of all the salmon in the world, the sockeye is by far the best to eat and fights every bit as well as even the dramatic silvers. It is an amazingly prolific fish in Alaska, and each year tens of millions of them ascend the rivers to spawn. Average size is something between six and eight pounds but ten- to fifteen-pound fish are not uncommon. The present Alaskan record is, however, well under twenty pounds.

In Alaska, mid-summer is the time to try for sockeye, and their very numbers make the fishing an experience of a lifetime. They might not be as massive as kings, but for sheer fun and thrills finding a sockeye run is certainly hard to beat.

The smallest of the Pacific salmon is the pink, but their numbers compensate for their size. Other names for the pink are humpback or humpy, but it is generally known as pink because its red/orange flesh turns pink when canned. The name humpback describes the grotesque hump that the males grow after entering fresh water. Again, most fish run during the summer and provide amazing sport on light tackle. Many in Alaska spin for them with just four-pound line. Round the Pacific coast fly fishing sea-water pinks is considered one of the greatest challenges. Very light, very short rods with small flies fished quickly seem to be favourite methods.

The final Pacific salmon is the chum, a fish that averages between ten and twelve pounds and runs the rivers of Alaska in particular slightly later on in the summer and even the autumn. These fish are greatly appreciated for extending the salmon season, for their spectacular fight and for their eating qualities.

It is undeniable that salmon anglers on the west coast of America enjoy some splendidly varied fishing. We probably think that the Atlantic salmon is the greatest of them all, but that should not blind us to experiences that many hundreds of thousands of anglers thoroughly enjoy. It could well be that a trip to the west coast would be handsomely rewarded, and there are adventures even further afield.

Mahseer

For around a century the mahseer was known as the Asian salmon. In fact, the mahseer is not a salmon at all and looks rather like a cross between a carp and a barbel. However, it was the best thing that the Anglo-Indians of 1850–1947 could find on the sub-continent, and they made the best of it they could, soon finding that mahseer are the best freshwater fish in the world bar none! They grow very large, and in the south of India ninety-pound fish are not uncommon. Even in the Himalayan rivers forty- and fifty-pound fish are quite possible, even today.

The mahseer can be considered a true game fish, and it will accept a fly every bit as gladly as it does a spinner, a fish bait or even a lump of paste. Whether or not you can actually land a mahseer on fly tackle is a completely different question, but there is no doubt that the mahseer is the best fighter in fresh water anywhere in the world. I myself have been on four journeys to India and Nepal hunting mahseer, and

A fantastic fifty-pound mahseer from the upper Ganges.

the first run cannot be compared with any other fish. The largest I have yet to land on a fly is sixteen pounds, and it took me just over an hour and a quarter of very bruising battle before it was landed. The fish are all magnificent. There are various sub-species: the gold, the silver and the black are my own favourites, and they lie in the Indian sun like fish gods.

Of course, mahseer fishing is unlike anything else. The rivers are always magical, and frequently you are fishing in the shadow of colossal, snow-capped mountains. Wherever you go, you attract whole villages of excited colourful children, gabbling behind you, fingering pieces of fishing tackle and carrying your camera, your camping gear or your food.

The season for mahseer differs greatly from one part of Asia to the next. Mounting a mahseer campaign takes months of effort and organization, and it would be utterly foolhardy to consider a trip before every little bit of homework has been done. India can be a dangerous and a frustrating place, but the mahseer is worth every ounce of sweat and frustration.

Huchen and Taimen

Finally, there are the huchen and the taimen, land-locked spring-spawning river fish that spread all across northern Asia even as far as Japan. The huchen is also found very rarely now in parts of Germany and Austria, particularly in tributaries of the Danube system. The huchen is the smaller of the two and grows to 'only' sixty pounds or so, whereas the taimen almost certainly tops a hundred pounds and there are old Japanese reports of fish to 150 pounds!

A very rare shot of a magnificent huchen of over forty pounds.

These are extraordinary fish, and I doubt whether there are more than a handful of British anglers who have caught either. The best chance of a huchen today is probably under the care of a Russian or German angler who really knows the rivers and the lies. Winter seems to be the best time for these fish, but it is certainly not possible to travel to eastern Europe with any real hope of success unless a great deal of preparation has been undertaken.

Exactly the same goes for the taimen, but with this larger species the geography is even more frightening. Most of the taimen are now to be found in Mongolia and Siberia, and often the rivers that they inhabit have never been fished at all by western Europeans.

A Dane, a great friend of mine, mounted an expedition for them in 1992, starting from Japan. He set out with several Land Rovers into Mongolia and travelled for weeks until he came to a river reputed to hold them. He began to catch smaller fish, exciting enough in themselves, but he found that the very largest fed at night. One particular memory entranced him more than any others. It was a night of a full moon, and the silvery rays bounced across the empty plateau and caressed the shining river. There was a hatch of large moths and large taimen were nosing up to sip them down as they floated through the pools. Accordingly, my Danish friend tied on large bushy dry flies and by the time the first rays of dawn began to slide across the planet, he had taken two fish of sixty-one pounds and fifty-six pounds – what a brace and what a magnificent reward for such a brave and fearless fisherman.

2 THE ESSENTIALS

FINDING SALMON FISHING

Here is the first and most crucial of all problems, one that many never really come to grips with: by and large, the more you pay for your salmon fishing, the better it is likely to be. This general rule is broken over and over again, I know, but there is still a strong enough element of truth in it to bear its repetition. Salmon fishing is not cheap today. It never really has been, and that is why it has often been seen as a sport of kings, princes and the aristocracy. Like it or not, fishing for salmon has always had upper-class overtones, and the price has had a great deal to do with that. Some of my friends have worked out the cost of each of their individual Scottish salmon, and it comes to thousands of pounds – a price way beyond the pocket of the man happy to fish for dace or roach.

Association Water

This notwithstanding, price should not necessarily put off the man keen to catch salmon, and there are relatively cheap ways to find access to passably good water. In most parts of the salmon fishing country, day tickets are available. Sometimes these can be bought from farmers and riparian owners, sometimes from inns, but generally from Associations. Indeed, Association water is often of the highest quality, and a weekly membership can often be obtained for a very reasonable sum. There is plenty of good Association water in Scotland and in Wales with good pools and good salmon runs at certain times of the year.

Of course, there are still problems with this type of fishing. In my experience, the Associations are dominated by the locals who know the river inside-out right down to every twig and stone on the bottom. The problem is obvious: you are competing against real experts on a water that you have probably never seen before in your entire life, and the odds are stacked very heavily against you. More than that, the locals will know exactly when to be out and where to fish the river under every conceivable condition. If a stranger catches a fish under the nose of the locals, then he is either extremely lucky or extremely skilful, and I personally have yet to manage the feat more than half a dozen times.

On certain Association waters, the locals are very friendly and do their best to help you along to some sport. In my experience this advice is confined to catching trout and grayling, and they keep the big boys for themselves, but I do remember some splendid times on the River Tummel with kind-hearted Scottish salmon anglers, so all is never lost if you are patient and ask in the right way.

Hotel Beats

In all probability the best and most accessible water for a man or woman relatively new to the sport can be found on hotel beats. There are many hotels throughout the UK that to a large extent have based their reputation on the quality of the salmon fishing that they offer. Many hotels control several miles of very good river indeed, and annual catches can be sky high. Best of all, the bulk of their water is usually reserved just for their guests. Therefore, there can be few local experts to whittle the fish away

Superb Scottish Association water.

from you; everybody starts with pretty much of an even chance as far as water knowledge goes. Another good thing about hotel fishing is that you will get every bit of help and encouragement you could possibly want. After all, it is in the hotel's best interest that you should go away a happy and contented customer, desirous of booking for the same fortnight the following year. If there is anybody in the hotel that can put you on to good salmon fishing, then you can be sure that he or she will come forward.

If there is a problem with hotel fishing then it is frequently the cost. The fishing itself might not be very expensive, but you have to take into account sizeable hotel bills. The vast majority of salmon hotels charges quite hefty weekly rates. They have to, for they have the fishing to

keep up, and they are often in remote locations. Still, providing you can afford it, there is little to beat relaxing in front of a large open fire after dinner with a good glass of port, after an excellent day's fishing with the sure knowledge of a comfortable and quiet bedroom above your nodding head!

Renting Stretches of River

More experienced salmon fishers will probably want to try and secure their own fishing on a more permanent basis, and the salmon fishers of old used to lease their waters. This practice began in Victorian days when gentlemen could spend several months each year, often fishing out the whole season. This type of lifestyle bred many of the great names of salmon fishing,

A classic stretch of the Tweed at Kelso, just below the Junction Pool, a place famous and beloved by all salmon anglers.

but sadly – with the speeding up of social and economic life – few men are able to do that now.

However, there are still many fortunate enough to rent stretches of prime river, and this is probably the surest way of securing excellent salmon fishing. The problems, though, are immense. Very often it is a case of stepping into dead men's shoes. Good beats are jealously guarded and usually handed down, father to son, so it is very difficult for a newcomer to break into the ranks. It is only by pestering the fishing agents, year in and year out, that a good new beat is likely to be secured. Believe me, I have tried for years myself, and the process requires real determination.

There are, none the less, just a few possibilities. In recent years the standard of salmon fishing, as we well know, has slipped in many areas, and some beats have come onto the market that have previously been booked up for decades. If you are willing to take a bit of a risk and go for a beat that appears to be on the way down, then you could eventually be in for something of a surprise when the river picks itself out of the trough. This has happened on the middle Wye. Many of the previously famous beats came onto the market at a very reasonable price. A friend of mine has snapped up two of these with long-term guarantees, and I have no doubt that in a few years he will reap some tremendous benefits.

Time-Share

The most recent and most controversial scheme to provide salmon fishing on a long-term basis is the time-share trade. The practice of letting beats out on time-share began in the 1980s when optimism, fish stocks and bank accounts were all high. Many flocked to secure a week or two each year for life even on well-known rivers. Very many purchasers were carried away by the name of the water or by the thought of a wise investment. Often very high prices were paid, which were soon to be regretted. By the turn of the decade the crash came. The economy went into recession, as did the salmon stocks. Bad fishing and bad trade seemed ready to destroy the time-share trade altogether, and by 1990 some companies were recording nil sales.

The salmon time-share trade enraged many. The fear was that classic salmon beats would be taken away from traditional ownership, let out to yuppies who could not be expected to understand the river. Time-share was seen as a cynical, capitalist way of destroying one of Britain's great heritages. Perhaps there was an element of truth in these fears, but by and large, nowadays, the considered opinion is that time-share might well be something of a saving grace for many of our rivers.

Ideally, the time-share operation should be very well organized and based on sound fishery policies. Salmon rivers – not just the classic ones – are now seen as serious economic possibilities and must, therefore, be managed as such. The old trend of stocking rivers artificially with salmon parr has been discredited. Very few survived to return as adult fish, and in any case the rivers were not being improved. Time-share companies have become increasingly aware of this and have started to look in much greater detail at the rivers themselves. Nowadays there is far greater emphasis on improving the pools, the fishing stations and especially the spawning redds. Once stocks at sea are not ravaged, a well-managed hospitable river will begin to produce salmon again in good numbers, the time-share punters will again be satisfied, and weeks will sell like proverbial hot cakes.

The advice of many agents, therefore, is to buy into time-share (if that is your wish) now, while prices are reasonably static. The chances are that towards the turn of the century salmon stocks and the market as a whole will be on the upturn, and prices will necessarily reflect that.

If you are a prospective time-share purchaser, the important thing is to realize that you are investing in pleasure and satisfaction for years to come and not for some monetary gain. That is where many of the early time-share punters slipped up. They lost money and became enraged. Once salmon fishing is seen in terms of pound notes, it is obviously devalued, and everybody knows deep down it is vital to keep this perspective. How can anybody put a price on a glorious river on a spring day, when the mountains are capped with snow, and big silver fish are stitching through the water in front of you?

Time-share has had some strange repercussions – not always beneficial for long-term riparian owners. I was recently told of a case on the lower Dee, of a beat that had never been considered much good for anything for many years. Then a time-share company took over, huts were built, access was improved and fishing stations erected. Because of the name of the river, weeks were quickly sold, even though the beat had never been highly regarded locally. Because of all this, its value rocketed to several million. This created a major problem for the elderly riparian owner just upstream. Suddenly his own beat (a much better one) that had been in his family for decades assumed a totally new value. In fact, it was now estimated to be worth something between two and three million pounds! How on earth can this be passed on through the family when the present owner dies? The death duties will be prohibitive. It is sad to think of a traditional ownership like this coming to an end.

Auctions

There are other, sometimes unexpected, wrinkles to locating excellent salmon fishing. Perhaps the nicest is the postal auction of fishings managed by the Atlantic Salmon Trust at Pitlochry. The idea is that owners all over the country put their beats up for postal auction for one or two days or even a week or more. This is a truly excellent way of gaining access to some of the most cherished fishing in the UK. I have the 1994 catalogue in front of me as I write. There are 213 lots in all, some expected to go for a little as sixty or seventy pounds. At the other end of the scale there are numerous beats on the Tweed, the Till, the Wye, the Usk, the Spey and the Naver. There is even the opportunity to rent lodges and make up a house party of a dozen or so. It is an excellent idea for all concerned and a super way to enjoy very varied fishing indeed.

TACKLE

House of Hardy

It would be totally wrong to say that the House of Hardy is the only manufacturer making good salmon tackle today, but it would be true that

for many generations the name and the product have gone hand in hand. Certainly, around many parts of the world, Hardy is still seen as the typical British company making high-class salmon rods, reels and accessories.

It all began in 1872 when the Hardy brothers decided to expand their cutlery business to include shooting and fishing equipment. By the turn of the century their firm had become the most progressive company in its field and perhaps the most famous fishing tackle maker in the world. The item that effected this rocket to fame was created in 1891 when the brothers introduced their first patented fly-reel. It was a brass, frameless centrepin reel with a simple wire line guide, but its drum ran on ball-bearings which reduced wear and friction. The reel was also fitted out with a ratchet and pull-check mechanism on which the braking tension could be adjusted. The Hardy catalogue made a great deal of these advances, and with the confidence typical of the Victorians the brothers named

A shot of the rod room at the old Hardy factory.

the reel model the Perfect. It became without doubt the most famous fly-reel in the world.

The Hardy Company did not restrict itself to reels, but built a whole range of fishing tackle, from accessories to the most important rods of the day. Hardy's marketing was also way ahead of its time, and the firm worked closely with the most famous anglers of the period to create rods that bore the true stamp of authenticity. Trout and coarse rods were all constructed to the requirements and designs of great men. So too were salmon rods. In 1914 the Wye rod was brought out. As usual, the Hardys recruited an expert to give his opinion on the rod, and in this case the commentator was the 'Napoleon of the Wye', Robert Pashley. The success of the Wye rods continued, and in 1926 the Hardys recruited the salmon sensation of the time A. H. E. Wood, who gave his name to a range of single-handed rods. So the story continues to this very day.

The House of Hardy still has its proud shop in Pall Mall just off St James, in London, a dignified building that has seen the start of so many salmon expeditions and perhaps even set men on the road to becoming salmon anglers for the rest of their lives. The shop is in one of the more genteel parts of the city, settled in between hatters and wine shops, and handy for the Ritz. The interior reflects this, with handsome displays, carpeting, an intelligent angler's book shelf and the type of gifts that you would happily give your hostess after a day on her husband's river. The staff are perfect for this environment and certainly know their stuff – about fish all over the world and most especially salmon. One of them is Terry Weldon, a man well known to me. He contacted me around four years ago before his own personal adventure to India after the Himalayan mahseer.

Terry's expedition was very much an epic one, and despite all the usual trials and tribulations he and his companions battled on, got to the river and found the fish. You can talk to Terry about everything, and there remains an underlying spirit of adventure in the whole shop today (witness the majestic stuffed tiger fish snarling on the wall!). It is interesting that Hardys used to be *the* manufacturer of mahseer gear, and you will find that the last remaining tackle shops around Asia proudly sport the Hardys logo, the great emblem of quality throughout the world.

I've already said that a good many companies make excellent tackle, but Hardys really is very good indeed, and you *know* that it will be right. The price might be high, but it is not prohibitive, and you have the good feeling that you are getting exactly what you are paying for. Let's have a look at what Terry Weldon advises his customers to buy.

Rods and Reels

Probably the number-one kit bought from Hardys would feature the 15ft 4in Hardy Deluxe salmon rod. This retails at around £450 but is truly magnificent. It takes a Number 10 line with ease and is just about perfect for any medium to large salmon river. This rod marries perfectly with the JLH reel, which can be bought for around £120. If your budget isn't quite up to that, you will want the Hardy Favourite – fifteen feet long and £369. This couples well with the Marquis Number 2 reel at around £80. It also takes a Number 10 line and is made on pretty much the same lines with the same materials as the Deluxe.

It could well be that you have already done a fair bit of trout fishing and have a meaty 10ft trout rod in your possession. If so, you will probably find that this will do well for most of the smaller west coast spate rivers, where single-handed rods are becoming more and more the rage, following in the excellent footsteps of the Americans who never saw the need for the fifteen-, sixteen- and seventeen-feet weapons. Check before setting out. If you are not on one of the wide, majestic classic rivers, it is quite likely that something smaller and lighter will do just as well.

Lines

Lines come in several designs and prices but most settle between £25 and £40. A floating line will probably do for most requirements, certainly throughout the summer. If you are contemplating big flies in deep fast water in very cold conditions, then you should be looking at one of the quick sink lines on offer. It will be vital if you are really going to get your fly down deep and put it where the fish will be waiting.

Other Items

There's not a great deal more to be said. Waders will be a necessity on virtually all rivers. These are increasingly made of neoprene, a new material introduced from America a few years ago sweeping the British market because of the vast warmth that it gives. However, they are not cheap at around £200; and most of us have made do with the ordinary rubber ones for many decades. If you are going to do a lot of spring fishing and the water is cold they might make sense.

You will obviously need some leaders, probably ready-made-up ones, nicely tapering about twelve feet in length and anything between twelve- and sixteen-pound breaking strain. You will want to buy a fly box at around £15. Whether or not you buy a net is rather up to you. A vast number of salmon are easily landed without one, but having a net with you does give a feeling of confidence. If £80 does not put you off, perhaps its a wise investment.

An essential investment, as far as I am concerned, is a priest – the heavily weighted stick with which you dispatch your prized salmon, if that is what you want to do in these difficult days of ours. Believe me, there is nothing worse than being an excited angler, wanting to kill a fish and looking around for the first available club-sized rock. It really is like having Neanderthal Man back on the river bank, and the rock does no favours to the salmon at all. Firstly, it is hardly ever properly balanced, and quite a

few blows will be needed to kill the fish. Secondly, if you are going to kill a fish, it would be nice to take one back that is barely marked rather than having the head badly cut and bruised. Also, think of the angler's image. Just imagine how it looks to any passer-by, walking the dog say, to see a man crouched over a fish, bashing it senseless, rock in hand. I need not elaborate any further.

After that, one only needs flies, and according to Terry the Hairwing doubles now dominate the market in all the classic patterns. In fact, of all the salmon flies Terry sells perhaps eighty per cent are of this design. However, he always recommends his customers to take some shrimp flies and trebles and, for early-spring and late-autumn fishing, some brass tube flies and Waddingtons.

There you have it – all the salmon fly fisherman is every likely to need. Of course, there are accessories you can build up over the years, but the basics are quite sufficient in themselves.

Tackle for Spinning

However, it could well be that you will also be wanting to do some spinning – very much a favourite method on the early rivers. There are many excellent light pike and light carp rods now on the market that make superb salmon spinning rods. These can be nicer and lighter in action than the rods designed specifically for salmon, and they are often a good deal cheaper. I really would check some of these out before making a decision.

The dogma of yesterday said that you had to spin for salmon with a multiplying reel. I don't quite know why this fallacy sprung up, but it is probably a relic from the 1920s when the fixed-spool reel began to appear and was somehow seen as cheating. This is nonsense: the fixed-spool reel is perfectly designed for salmon fishing and is much easier to control than a multiplier. Admittedly, a multiplier looks and sounds good, but if you get into a bird's nest on a windy, frosty, sleeting day in Scotland,

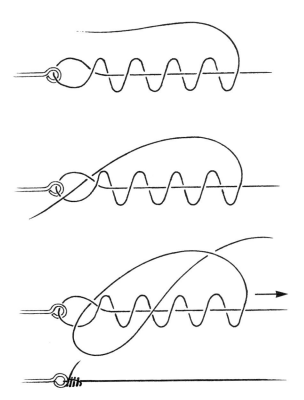

The tucked half blood knot. This is the knot I always use for spinners, swivels and straight-eyed hooks. It has never let me down so far to my knowledge.

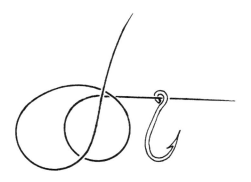
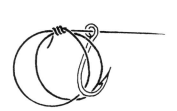

The two-circle, two-turn Turle knot. This is an extra-strong knot for salmon flies.

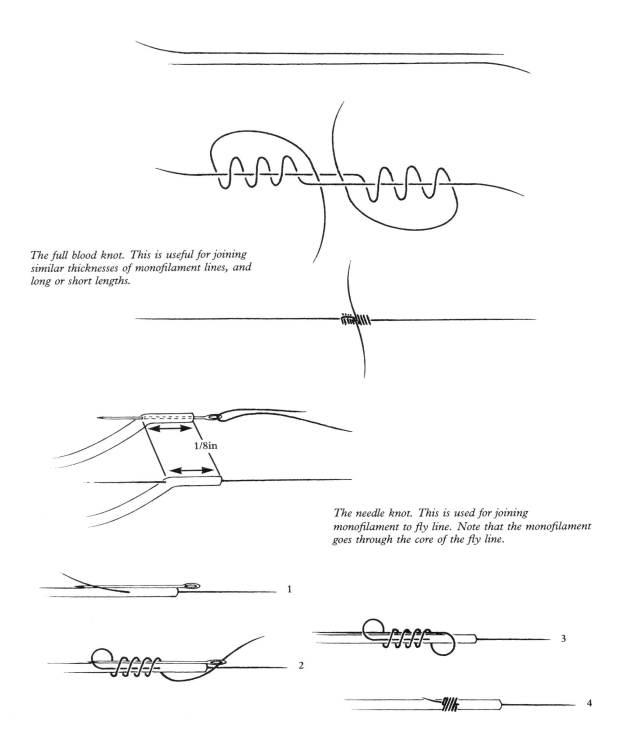

The full blood knot. This is useful for joining similar thicknesses of monofilament lines, and long or short lengths.

1/8in

The needle knot. This is used for joining monofilament to fly line. Note that the monofilament goes through the core of the fly line.

1

2

3

4

you'll wish you'd never seen the damned thing! For what it is worth, my own opinion is that Shimano makes the best fixed-spool reels today, with a tremendous size range – one of which is bound to suit your rod and the river perfectly.

As a final consideration, how about one of the beautifully light American spinning rods that are now imported into this country by Chris and Sue Harris in Norfolk? These are little wands of things, only five to six feet in length and weighing a handful of ounces. They might not be nearly enough for the big, rolling classic rivers, but I imagine they would be terrific for the spate streams where accuracy of casting is all. Just imagine what a fabulous battle you would get from a grilse or even a small salmon on such a tool. This type of rod really could help spinning be recognized as the art form it truly is.

FLIES

Putting together a first salmon fly box can be a very problematic and expensive affair. If you walk into any well-stocked tackle shop, especially in Scotland, the array of salmon flies that stares out at you can be overwhelming. They come in all shapes, sizes, colours and materials, and some have single hooks or double hooks or are mounted on trebles. To buy one of everything on display would cost a fortune and you would need a travelling case to carry it all about, so just where does one begin putting the first few flies together?

First of all, choosing salmon flies is far easier than building up a trout fly collection. When you are trout fishing you are trying to imitate the actual insect upon which the fish is feeding at that particular moment in time, and as there are thousands of insects that make up the trout diet, it stands to reason you are going to need an awful lot of flies through the course of a season. Add to that the list of various lures and traditional wet flies, and the trout fisherman really does have a headache.

Fly tying is one of the oldest of arts.

Salmon flies are different in that they do not make the same attempt to resemble food forms. They – generally, if not always – are created on a whim or around a theory, with no real natural pattern. Flies are whipped up and used, and if the river gods are kind and the flies are successful, they will be used again. Success breeds success, and eventually the pattern enters angling lore and possibly your fly box. Thus, while there is a very good reason why a trout takes a pheasant-tail nymph, the success of salmon men with the Green Highlander, for example, defies explanation.

There are four major considerations when picking out salmon flies – or so I was told when I was assembling my first fifty flies or so.

Size

The first consideration is going to be size, and this is heavily dependent on the water temperature and the time of the year. In general terms, the colder and murkier the water, the bigger the fly should be; the warmer and clearer the water, the smaller it should be. For this reason, for example, if you are fishing water that is forty degrees Fahrenheit or below, then a fly of around three inches in length is probably called for. As the water temperature climbs, let us say to forty-five degrees, then you can scale the fly down to two or two and a half inches. Once the water temperature is in the fifties, things change dramatically and you might be looking at a fly tied on hooks size 4–8. If the water becomes warmer still, let's say fifty-five to sixty degrees, you are looking at flies between sizes 6 and 10.

That is a very rough guide indeed – one that has been postulated in many books and articles and handed down by more grandfathers than I could begin to count – yet it seems to hold good. Of course, there are a great number of contradictions to it. One of the first Devon salmon I ever caught was in a very warm summer flood on a fly two and a half inches long. Equally, one spring when I was grayling fishing on the Tweed, I caught a lovely eight-pound fresh-run fish on a size 12, so you never really can tell, and generalizations are only a part of the fun!

Colour

We now come to the question of colour, and as some of the fly collections in our tackle shops make the hat collection at Harrods look pretty dull by comparison, it is not an easy choice. Actually, I am very far from convinced that salmon pay any heed to colour whatsoever. I think they probably see colours in quite different tints and hues anyway. However, there are rough guides. Whenever the water is clear, I have always been recommended to use a fairly sombre fly that does not look too out of place in the water. If the water is very murky indeed for some reason – generally floodwater of course – then a rather more colourful fly is needed to stand out from all the silt, sediment and floating rubbish. This is really the only time that I use startlingly colourful flies, and my own aim is to try to pick the colour to merge in with the water clarity as much as possible. You will sometimes find that rivers run with certain tints to them, and if possible I like to match the fly to the water it is swimming in.

I had one particular experience when I was fishing for trout in Kashmir that supports this theory. One of the rivers that we set about came straight from the glacier and ran a deep blue in colour. My old salmon fishing experience came back to me, and after a couple of unsuccessful hours, I moved to a wet fly that I had tied some time before using several blue feathers in it. I'm not going to say I emptied the river, but at least I began to get takes and land the odd fish.

Dressing

The third consideration is the dressing of the fly. Older patterns of salmon fly were generally dressed with feathers, and if you watch them work in the water they somehow look stiff and unnatural. I know that our angling grandfathers caught great numbers of salmon on these patterns, so they cannot be all bad but, then again, perhaps there were more salmon in the rivers with far less pressure on them. Today, I am far happier fishing a fly tied – wherever possible – with hair of some sort, perhaps from a squirrel or a goat.

One of the tube flies designed by Richard Waddington many years ago demonstrates this perfectly. If you let this swim in the water beneath you, you will see that it works beautifully, and if anything represents a small fish, it is this amazing fly. Indeed, I have had great success with Waddington tube flies when fishing for pike – and pike can be very discriminating. By contrast, I have had no success pike fishing when using salmon flies tied with feathers.

As far as I am concerned, the amount of dressing, too, is important. I just do not like flies that are overly made up, and I prefer those that are as sparsely dressed as possible. Again, in my view, this is all to do with the natural swimming position of the fly in the water.

Of course, when you are looking at that great board of salmon flies in an angling shop, it can be very difficult to work out in your mind just which will swim nicely and tantalizingly. Perhaps the best idea is to buy a few of those that fit the guide lines so far and see how they look in the water, then build up your collection from there.

Intended Depth

The fourth consideration when choosing flies is the depth at which they will work. The colder the water is, the deeper you want the fly to move, and when temperatures are below forty-five degrees, I really like to fish the fly as deep as possible, possibly even touching bottom from time to time. For this, again, the Waddington tube flies are excellent creations. You can work them along, very slowly, almost feeling them rubbing along the bottom silt and debris.

As the water warms, you will be wanting to fish with a floating line and a lighter fly that swims somewhere in the surface layers. Indeed, there are those that actually like their salmon flies to create a 'V' as they swing round on the current. Obviously, this means that for warmer water fishing you will be looking at flies that are lighter and will sink less quickly.

Hook

At this point we have to look at the question of the hook the fly is tied upon. In all probability, the big flies of the spring and the cold water are going to be tied on trebles or at least double hooks. As the water warms, single and double hooks – for me, anyway – begin to take over. I have watched a great many small flies tied on small treble hooks in the water, and I do not like the way that they swim. They often look a little bit lopsided, and the hook can pull them off the horizontal in a depressingly unreal way. I know that in theory it should be easier to hook a salmon with a treble, but I am not convinced. With the smaller flies, certainly smaller than size 8, I am nowadays quite happy to use a single hook, and my catch rate has not suffered at all.

Local Knowledge

I would like to add a fifth, informal, consideration: local knowledge and advice. Whenever I fish a water new to me, one of my first jobs is to ask the owner, the gillie, fellow fishermen or the local tackle dealer what flies they recommend and use. I am totally humble and sincere in this. It is their river, and they should know far better than any newcomer. If I'm lucky, they will pass on a little bit of their knowledge. It very often happens that two or three people agree on the same selection of flies, and these are the ones I make sure to carry, at first anyway. Local knowledge is not always right, but it would be arrogant to ignore it, and it does give you a little bit of confidence when you are starting out. It should not blinker you to your own experience, nor should it stop you thinking for yourself if things are not going well, but it is an important consideration that anybody would be stupid to ignore.

It is important to care for your fly collection once it has begun to build up. At the end of the season it is all too easy to put your fly box away wet and ill-sorted and leave it in a shed till the following spring. It is far better to take the flies home after every trip. Take them indoors, open the lid and let them dry out in a warm environment. Most salmon flies are very tough, but points do rust and weaken, and it would be idiotic not to keep them in first-class condition. After all, the hook point is the most critical piece of tackle: if it lets you down, you are another salmon worse off.

COURSES FOR THE SALMON ANGLER

It is an old adage but none the less an absolutely true one that personal tuition is worth more than thousands upon thousands of words – especially when it comes to the physical acts of casting or pointing out lying fish. For many years fishing courses have flourished, particularly since the face of salmon fishing has changed a great deal and fathers and grandfathers are not playing the same dominant role in teaching youngsters that perhaps they once did. One of the most famous schools was run formerly by a father-and-son team, John and Simon Gawesworth down in Devon; more recently, Simon has taken over the reins entirely and has continued to attract some excellent attention. Here, the editor of *Salmon and Trout* *Magazine* undergoes the Gawesworth experience:

The Gawesworth School

I went not to receive instruction, being by now far too old, stupid and set in my ways to profit much by it, but to learn something of the art of imparting it to more deserving cases, also of the evolving mood and responses of those who go there to be crash-coursed into fly fishers, competent enough to catch fish and embark thereafter on a further programme of judicious self-improvement.

That is not to say that the intake is confined to absolute tyros. Anglers who have muddled along for years tangling nylon and flopping line in loops on the water all-too-immediately before them every third or fourth cast also submit themselves to be put through the

Fishing the River Spey.

Gawesworth mill. They come out on the far side better and more confident men or women. Courses are small – four, five or six pupils – to facilitate individual tuition. There are several options, structured to meet a variety of demands. A week is the customary duration.

Ours began at 6 p.m. on a Saturday early in August. Introductions were made all round, followed by an appetising dinner, and then we were under starter's orders. Beginning-of-term nerves inhibited appetites, and serving dishes went back to the kitchen bearing visible traces of their erstwhile contents for what was to be the only time that week.

What next? We put our feet up in the sitting room for a bit, watching a spot of telly while tobacco smoke and alcohol expedited digestion? Not on your life. Casting champion Simon, stern and determined for his years, ushered his elders, contemporaries and juniors to the ground-floor lecture room and started instruction by asking, then telling them, what a fly rod is, a reel and a line. Nothing is taken for granted. His style calls to mind a pleasant young monk to whom God has spoken directly, mildly spreading enlightenment among the less favoured. He does it with exceptional lucidity and not a shade of pretension.

Then knots! What a good idea that was. Tying knots improperly loses anglers more fish than any other single ineptitude. Cushion to backing, backing to line, line to leader, but why use a nylon leader? Just because we cannot poke the tip of a fly-line through the eye of a typical fly-hook, perhaps? Now we arrive in radical, even revolutionary, territory. None will go the S.G.S.F.F. (Simon Gawesworth School of Fly Fishing) in danger of hearing only that which is already familiar. Tuition techniques having been refined by long practice. Knots may be demonstrated initially by use of plastic tubing and string, but not for long. Pupils are soon at it, their artefacts being offered for eagle-eyed scrutiny by monk Simon. There is kindly sympathy for clumsiness and remarkable patience with it, but no abatement of standards. The fumble-fingered struggle on until successful. None wishes it otherwise, and the clock strikes 10.30

p.m. before we stagger off to our comfortable bedrooms and beds.

First light on Sunday shows those who see it a grey, wet and windy sky, a drenched landscape and a risen river running coloured. A day indoors, one supposes. No. Unfishable the Torridge may be, but not unwadeable. We dress up in the waterproofs we have been told to bring and don loaned waders if necessary. Loaded with assembled tackle, we journey down to the School's water below and splash one after the other into its racing current under careful supervision. The cold water in our waders can only help to teach what this sport is all about. Strung out, standing in the safer stations, we attempt the impersonation of our patterns. Surprisingly, to one who has been watching this sort of thing for thirty-five years, the impersonations are soon recognizable. There is clearly more than meets the eye immediately in the Gawesworth method.

Before the day is out, the class has advanced beyond overhead toing and froing. Those promising aptitude are on to roll and switch casting, an area in which I find there is more to be learned than I fancied and more hope than was foreseen of learning some of it. Ye Gods! I actually send one or two across to the bankside bushes. With a fly on the end and low water, one of them might have induced a take.

Simon, putting us all into perspective at the end of the day, rolls one across the full width of the river, dropping leader-tip on water running about two feet below the lowest willow branches swaying in the gusting wind.

Lunch had been frugal, only the manners of a lifetime's ingraining saved dinner plates from a final polish with the tongue. There had been a whole roast turkey to carve for ourselves. Then to the visitors' sitting room to watch oneself on video film and hear again the comments, at times pithy, of the patient but not necessarily ceremonious instructors.

Day's end at last? No. It was back downstairs to the lecture room to complete the story of the knot (leader to fly) and to learn more of the fly itself and the hooks on which flies are dressed. Learning rates were then tested by brief and painless written examination. It was 11 p.m. before we broke up for the evening,

Simon Gawesworth teaches his pupils to Spey cast the Single Spey.

replete, content and fascinated, self-confidence bursting from bud to leaf.

Monday started with theory and ended with more, sandwiched around the reality. We travelled to Exe Valley Fishery, also tainted by flood, for an afternoon's practical work. The rainbow trout were not, in that water, as suicidally inclined as some of us had been led to expect, yet all but one of the party had at least one fish. The best was three and a half pounds.

Most discovered, as the instructors had anticipated and confided to me, that it is very easy to forget all one has painstakingly learned once there is a fly on the leader and trout showing in the water. However, a fish caught is a fish caught, no matter how inelegantly. One student learned the hard way that it is better to priest the fish aimed at than the butt of the adjacent rod.

The final lesson that day was how to gut a trout for the deep freeze. Here, those already adept were at liberty to aid those who were not. There was no lecture that evening. We relaxed with a whisky we had procured en route for Dulverton and a video film on the dressing of flies (not part of this course) and their effective use on both still and running water.

Tuesday was given over to casting revision and an introduction to the double-handed salmon rod. The evening lecture developed into a controlled discussion centred on anglers' fads and fallacies. Those with experience were welcome to advance their own notions, a few to be embodied in future tuition, more to be dismantled, inspected and consigned to the scrap yard. Such was the enthusiasm that Simon sat with me for two hours after the official day closed at 11 p.m. for a further exchange of theories.

Wednesday took us to a harder stillwater

fishery, Bakewell, where I hooked but one fish – a beauty – only to see it throw the fly during the third hour of leaping. Others with fifty years' less general fishing experience brought their brace safely to the net. The best scaled $3\frac{3}{4}$ and $4\frac{3}{4}$ pounds. They came to a fly fished on a sunken leader only two feet in length. Colleges being by definition establishments where research and instruction go hand in hand, the Simon Gawesworth School of Fly Fishing could justify a change of title.

Continuing rain somewhat frustrated Thursday's plan and Friday's. Half the party was to fish the Taw on either day; the other half was to fish the little Yeo for its small, quick-on-the-trigger brownies. Two salmon were hooked but came adrift in the Taw's high water soon after the take; sea trout pulls were felt but not converted. Most of the Yeo's brownies were hugging the pebbles. Those which snatched the fly racing by kicked free on the way to the net. Mornings began with tackle assembly and guidance on the tactics for the day. Evening lectures were by this time optional but well attended. A modicum of fly dressing was finally thrown in for goodwill.

On Saturday morning I bade farewell to a group of new and valued friends. They were tackling-up for a final accompanied assault on another population of stillwater trout, those at Stafford Moor. At 6 p.m. the untiring Gawesworths were to receive and start work on a new intake. You don't get so tired doing the things you really enjoy. That, no doubt, is what give the course its subtle and unforgettable flavour. All the students whose education I had observed, and to some extent shared, told me before we parted that they might be encountered there again next year doing a refresher course, if only because they had enjoyed the first one so much.

Fishing and casting being what they are, there is no solid consensus on what in unquestionably correct and what is not. What is taught here verges occasionally on the eccentric, employing that term in its strictest meaning: out from the centre. On one or two minor points I retain reservations, but two things are sure. Firstly, the Gawesworths put out a spectacular length of line with exceptional elegance, especially in the more advanced fields of the art. That this is not my judgement alone is confirmed by a sideboard of tournament trophies threatening the floor beneath it with its excessive weight. Secondly, anyone wishing to start game fishing or any practitioner dissatisfied with his or her present performance, might do far worse than make a booking and put himself or herself in the capable Gawesworth hands. If willing and able to benefit from instruction, one is likely to emerge at the end, ready to take the road which leads to joining the ten per cent that accounts for ninety per cent of the salmon and trout caught.

Oglesby and Falkus

Simon Gawesworth is not the only instructor of distinction in the country. For many years indeed, Arthur Oglesby has been running his own courses at the Seafield Lodge Hotel, Grantown-on-Spey. I have not been to these courses myself, but I have spoken to many who have, and they have been uniformly in absolute favour. I have known Arthur for several years and always look forward to every single meeting with him. As far as I am concerned, he epitomizes just about the best of everything in fishing, whether it be game, sea or coarse. There just could not be a nicer, more knowledgeable, more unassuming man, and I should think to be taught by him would be one of the most pleasurable fishing experiences possible.

Then, of course, there is Arthur's old chum and partner Hugh Falkus – the great one, the majestic presence of Crag Cottage. The first time I met Mr Falkus was in 1988 when I visited him at his fishing school. I had read his books and seen his films, and I was prepared to be impressed but not mesmerized, as I was. For weeks afterwards, all I could really think of was Falkus. His words and his image seemed burned into me, and I really did feel that I had been in touch with whatever genius there might be in fishing.

So impressed was I with what I saw at Hugh Falkus' fishing course that I immediately put pen to paper:

It was in his role as teacher that I met Hugh Falkus for the first time. It was midsummer and very warm when I found his valley. The Lake District I always thought of as a hectic, teeming place, but not here beneath mountains, clad in forest and under the clear blue sky. I walked a stretch of his river and though I found it much shrunken in that drought period, I soon saw its potential. In a very deep pool, seven sea trout were lying. As far as I could see, three were good fish, three were big fish, and one was enormous. This was my first sight of his river! I passed his cottage; it was old, romantic and remote, clinging to the south face of the hillside. I carried on past it down the lane to a farmhouse where amidst duck flights I met him, teaching his pupils, Mr Mavin and Mr Stephen, to cast.

For half the afternoon, I watched them. Once I was a teacher myself, and I can appreciate a good one when he stands before me. Falkus has all the skills. Firstly, he casts so brilliantly well, all you want to do is copy him. He is like Sergeant Troy from Thomas Hardy's *Far From the Madding Crowd* when he is practising his sword play around Bathsheba Everdene. The sixteen-foot rod was a blur when he cast, bending, cutting and dancing through the air. Forty yards of line were aerialized, arcing, floating and arrowing over the water. He stood there like Moses with his staff, commanding the water, framed in spray and sunlight. The poise, the grace, the timing and the carefully controlled power were the inspiration every teacher has ever sought to give.

Not that Falkus revelled in it for simple display. No. He taught Mavin and Stephen through his every move, demonstrating and explaining his grip on the rod, the position of his feet, the angles, the loops and the timings that were all so necessary. He made complete and utter sense of that so frequently misunderstood physical action, spey cast.

I don't doubt that if you visit Mr Falkus and enrol on his course you will be as impressed as I was and learn even more.

Naturally, Messrs Falkus, Oglesby and Gawesworth are not the only gentlemen to give excellent tuition: more names and contacts are given in the notes (see pages 152–3). All I can do is urge you, if you are not totally experienced or confident, to think seriously about going on a course. As I said in the introduction to this section, one-to-one teaching is probably the answer to any problem.

PLAYING A SALMON

This excerpt is taken from Colonel North Dalrymple-Hamilton's own book *Red Letter Days*.

A day of days, or rather a night of nights, as in the far north regions of Scandinavia it is hard to tell night from day – The Land of the Midnight Sun. The scene is at Vina on that most wonderful of rivers the Alton... I started operations at a pool called Bollo, a small place, only about twenty casts but one that hardly ever failed to produce a fish or two every time I fished it. Little did I know what was in store for us. I fished down to where the river became dub-like and was just going to give it up when the wonderful happened. I remember the cast well. I'd pulled out some extra line, and I threw the fly right across the river into the deep slack water. I then proceeded to put my rod point into the little stream there which caught the line and drew the line across the deeper, still part of the river much quicker. Just as the line was straightening, out came a thing like a submarine with a tremendous wallop. I nearly fell into the river I was so astonished, and Anton who was half asleep in the stern woke up with a bang thinking a rock had fallen into the river. Old August said 'Stor Lax, I think', and I said nothing. The fish kept very quiet for a while but sank very deep. Realizing we were in a bad strategical position, I asked him to take the canoe across the other side. This was to get between the fish and a large sunken boulder in the river. Our going across upset the fish, and he went off like an express train, the reel fairly screaming, away, away, went line and backing. We were after it as hard as we could go, the line cutting the water into showers of spray. I began to have unpleasant visions of a trip into

Nedre Sierra down a very nasty rapid with numerous big boulders, and so did August who kept saying 'Must no leave pool'. That was all jolly fine but how to stop him? Over two hundred yards of line were out and going all we knew. Mercifully at the tail of the pool the fish stopped. I was very gentle with him. Slowly, very slowly I began to lead him upstream, bit by bit getting back a certain amount of line. By dint of great caution and gentleness I coaxed him away from the tail of the pool and suddenly he made up his mind to pay a visit to the head of the pool. Off he went right away to the very head in one agonizing rush. Luckily my big Corbet reel held the best part of three hundred yards of backing. Away we went after him. He didn't remain long in the strong water but turned and came back into the deep hole where he was first hooked. Here he began cruising about very deep but soon got bored with this and made another rapid excursion up to the head of the pool again and back to his deep hole. The next move was a rush down to the tail, where he played the big fish trick of crossing over, drowning the line and coming upstream at ten thousand miles an hour. This was an anxious moment as I had an enormous amount of slack and I was terrified it would all come away with a bang and snap the cast. I went downstream after the bend in the line, keeping the rod point down and things held. He was beginning to tire, and August wanted to land and get him into quiet water. I refused as I dreaded the inevitable rush he would make when he felt the water shoaling so he kept the boat in deep still water. The fish meantime was cruising about deep down, and we could not see him. By degrees he began coming up and up, and we began to get very excited as the cast began to show and then the fish. He looked enormous and I told Anton to gaff him as near the tail as he could but on no account to try until he was certain of getting him. At this he was splendid and as cool as a cucumber. The end came with dramatic suddenness. The fish slowly came to the surface, gave a slow heave, came half out of the water and lay still, dead beat. Anton put the clip in and we had him, although we did have a job getting him into the canoe. Being gaffed

near the tail he kept sliding along the gunwale. Then to shore, where by the aid of putting the ring of my weighing machine through the canoe pole, hoisting it onto the men's shoulders we got him weighed: a shade over fifty-eight pounds. Then pandemonium broke loose, and we behaved like children.

If you look hard enough I believe this piece just about sums up most of the rules for playing a big fish and quite obviously Dalrymple-Hamilton had enormous experience of monster salmon. Anyway, let's have a closer look at those rules in a rather more dry, logical way.

Remain Hidden

Firstly, it is vital to try to avoid being seen by the salmon as much as possible. Very many big fish of all species will not immediately realize there is danger on first being hooked. The pressure on them is unnatural, but that does not necessarily mean that they associate it with danger, and they are very likely to come close to the bank or to the boat with little opposition. However, once they see the angler or the boat then the fireworks are likely to begin. The longer that you can remain hidden from the fish, the more subdued the fight is likely to be. It is also very important to remain as inconspicuous as possible when it comes to the final landing stage of the battle: it is surprising how many fish can summon up energy for a last rush if the sight of a looming angler alarms them. A tired hook-hold or a frayed line might just give at this very last moment, so take no chances and remember just how sharp the salmon's eyesight can be.

Keep Calm

A second rule is to keep calm and not to panic in any way. This is easier said than done if you know you have a fish on, and it is trying to leave the pool. Still, if you lose your head, you will lose your fish; of that there is no doubt. I remember one particular Barle salmon that made me look a total, utter fool and should, by rights, have escaped easily.

I was trout fishing at the time on the upper beats of the Tarr Steps water when, quite out of the blue, a good-sized grilse snapped a floating fly down. Before I knew it, my tiny two-piece rod was bent like a reed in the storm, and I was attached to a fish far too big for me, the tackle and the river in a quite shrunken state. I panicked; I make no excuse. The fish reached the tail of the pool, and I did everything wrong so over it went and I was forced to follow, clattering my way down the dry, bleached summer falls after the fish. My fly-line got caught round rock after rock, and the rod finally got caught in a tree. In the end all the line had gone, and the backing, and the poor fish found itself still hooked and marooned in a tiny pool. I could wade in and scoop it onto the shore. Only right at the end did I exert any measure of self-control and that just saved a day that should have been lost.

By contrast, if you keep your head, virtually anything can be solved – broken lines, fish going through weirs – anything, providing you keep cool and think things out.

Be Positive

Thirdly, exert that coolness from the very moment the fish is hooked. Hugh Falkus – and many other experts – advise 'walking' a fish as soon as it is on. To do this you simply hold the rod at right angles to the river and walk smoothly, slowly, and steadily upriver. The chances are that the fish, quite puzzled, will follow, and you will be able to lead it out of danger and away from any shoal members. There is also a belief that walking a fish somehow exerts the angler's superiority and demoralizes the salmon in a strange way. Certainly, a fish that has been walked does fight with considerably less fury than one that has not. There are some salmon that simply dig in and will not come, and it is futile to force them. This, as I say, is a crucial point and you must know when a fish is asserting itself from the very start. Sometimes the fish will just turn and run, and to try and stop or walk it in these circumstances is to ask for an inevitable break-off. With a running fish you simply have to let it go – though hopefully not over the tail of the pool and into the rough water beneath, where you really will be in trouble. Make a fish work for every yard of line that it takes from you by putting on the maximum pressure that your tackle will stand. Remember that you really want to slow that run down and tire the fish, so you must make it pull for every inch of line.

It is vital to know when and how to put the pressure on a fish. During a run you will begin to sense that the fish is slowing down and perhaps tiring. At this point you must begin to increase the pressure noticeably. Hopefully the fish will come to a dead stop. It might rise in the water and even splash on the surface – a dangerous moment this, and one to be avoided if at all possible, by keeping the rod low. Obviously, you must know pretty accurately what your tackle will withstand in terms of pressure, and you must not be afraid to go to these limits. Very often you see a timid angler playing a fish with a rod only half bent: the length of the battle will be increased immensely like this and the chances of a hook pulling free are all the greater. Be confident in your tackle and really go for it in the fight. Do not let the salmon dominate, or you will be lost.

Pumping

A serious problem is a big fish that settles out in mid-stream where the water is quick and deep. It can seem immovable, and you might think that the fish has gone and you are hooked to the bottom. This is very probably not the case, and once you feel just the dullest kick you will know that you are still hooked in. This is where the art of pumping comes in. Take hold of the rod, up from the butt around the first eye, and pull gently but firmly upwards. As soon as your rod is vertical or even a little over your shoulder, wind in as you lower the tip towards the water. Repeat this process as often

Playing a big fish on spinning tackle and trying to keep it from the rapids.

as you can, and you will find that the salmon very gently moves towards you, hardly aware of what is going on. Finally, it will spark into life and the open fight will be rejoined. Pumping is an art – practised by every single big fish man – so try to learn it, and trust in it thoroughly.

Be Aware

Keep your eyes wide open during the fight, and do not develop tunnel vision for your rod and where the line enters the water. Rather, keep scanning around, looking for potential snags that could prove dangerous in the later stages of the fight. Try to be aware of patches of slack water where you might position a boat or try to lead a fish. Also, be aware of any possible sandy, shelving landing areas that you can begin to make for when the fight looks to be drifting towards its end. A good salmon fisherman is aware not only of what is going on down the line, but also of what is happening all round the pool.

Landing the Fish

Once you get to the landing stage of the battle, excitement is at its height. For my own part, I do not own a gaff any more and would never again sink a point of steel into a beautiful fish. Why spoil it? There is always a chance that you might want to return the fish for one of many reasons. Also, a gaff in inexperienced hands can be a disaster. It is far, far better to use a large landing net, and now that these are available with carbon-fibre frames, weight is absolutely no problem.

Over the last few years, I have seen very large mahseer and sturgeon landed by hand in Asia and Russia, and I now have no fear of going out for any fish without a net. In fact, the last score or so of salmon that I have landed have all been led into shallow water and beached on sand, gravel or grass. The process is quite simple: once the fish is tired and on its side, you simply lead it quickly but firmly into shallow water and keep the pressure on until it is

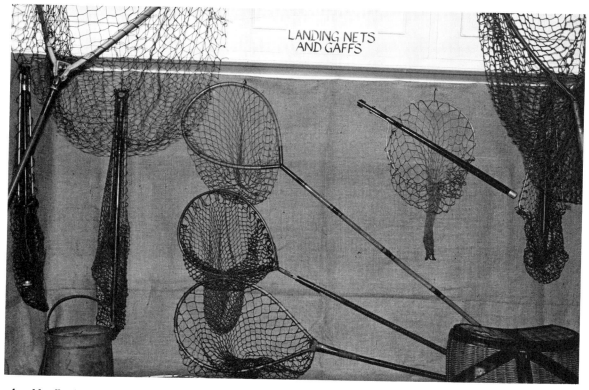

An old collection of stately landing nets – far better than the gaff.

on its side and half-beached. Put down the rod if the fish is big, and with both hands grip it close to the gills and slide it further up onto the grass. I have never felt in any danger of losing a fish of any size using this technique, and the only time that it is not possible is if you are fishing precipitous, sheer-sided rocky pools. The added advantage of this method is that the fish does not struggle nearly as much as it does in a net. This is important if you want to put the fish back, as you simply have to unhook it and slide it back the way it came. If a fish has wriggled and squirmed in a net, you may find that a stray hook has caught it in the side or perhaps the line has become tangled up in the mesh. It can take minutes to sort these things out, and all the time the fish is suffering.

Safety Precautions

There is one piece in Dalrymple-Hamilton's account that I omitted at the start: throughout the battle he was worrying about the state of his tackle, which he had rather carelessly left unchecked. This certainly increased the tension and made his relief all the greater when the huge fish was landed, but the risk was enormous. Always, always make sure that your line, knots and hook points are as strong and secure as they can be. Check everything frequently and leave nothing to chance. That way, during any fight, you will know that things are firmly stacked in your favour.

It is absolutely extraordinary the size of fish that can be landed on secure salmon tackle. I mentioned sturgeon a few lines ago, and in April 1993 I witnessed a beluga of nearly three

Satisfactory conclusion or sad end?

hundred pounds being played and eventually landed on only average salmon tackle. The fight did take three hours and at times the line and seventy yards of backing was out, but even a huge, tail-walking fish like this could not break free. Throughout, Neils, the Danish angler kept a cool head and obeyed all the rules mentioned above. After only thirty minutes, I think we all knew which way the fight would go.

If you hook a fish when wading, always remember that the first priority is to get yourself to the bank onto hard ground. It is virtually impossible to play a big fish when you are struggling in heavy water. Wading itself is a hazardous operation – or can be. Never get into water that makes you afraid. If you feel that you are getting beyond your depth or into water that is too fast, then retreat. I don't actually use one, but many find a wading stick useful. They are certainly worth investigating if you know you will be spending much time in deep, fast water.

You should also make sure that you wear a buoyancy aid of some sort (many are now built into fishing vests and the like) just as you would when out boat fishing. Then, should anything happen whilst you are out wading, you will be relatively safe if you relax, remember to keep your head up and drift with the current until slack water is reached.

I have not mentioned the use of a tailer in this chapter because I have never used one and do not like to comment. However, a tailer does seem to avoid the obvious problems with gaffs and nets, even if it does take a good deal of practice to wield one efficiently, and judgement is needed to decide on the exact moment to slide the noose up the fish and how far it should go so there is sufficient weight to set off the release and let the wire bite before reaching the tail itself. There are some other problems too: I am told, for example, that grilse are difficult to tail because of their slim shape and light weight and that sea trout have too thick a tail-wrist to let the noose work properly. Indeed, I have heard of big sea trout lost right at the bank because a tailer would not operate.

CASTING

By and large, casting a bait or a spinner is not particularly difficult, especially if a fixed-spool reel is used, although there can be problems with multipliers if the bait is light. However, we move into quite a different area when it comes to casting a fly – an integral part of salmon fishing for most people, for most of the year. There is no doubt at all that good fly casting does mean good fishing, and most salmon anglers will want to master the overhead cast, the roll cast, the side cast and the Single and Double Spey casts.

The first three casts are taken from the general world of fly fishing, and most emergent salmon fishers will have done their fair share of trouting anyway, and so should be able to make the transition to a longer rod and a heavier line without a great deal of difficulty or upset. It is the rather more specialized casts that cause grief – especially the Spey cast and to be a good Spey caster really does put you a little ahead of the field.

Strangely, I've often used Spey casting in a smaller way for trout fishing, especially on streams where bankside vegetation proves a problem; as a result, I have been able to make a transition to heavier rods and lines, but I do not say for a moment that I cast nicely or in anything like a conventional way. Whenever an expert sees me, I feel his inward groans, and I'm always promising to go on a course to be told where I'm going wrong and how I should improve – one such as those offered by Arthur Oglesby, Hugh Falkus or Simon Gawesworth. Simon writes here:

Special Casts

Spey Cast

'Occasionally, through necessity, a new cast is born – like the Spey cast, now widely recognized and used, which was developed through the need to cast a fly across the river, changing direction from downstream without catching the trees and bushes behind. The Double Spey is a simiiar cast. It is, however, commonly thought that you should use the Single Spey on the left bank and the Double Spey on the right bank (if you're a right-handed caster). As any competent Spey caster will tell you, the main reason for using a Double Spey in preference to the Single Spey is a wind blowing downstream, regardless of which hand you use or which bank you are standing on. As they say, 'all the Ds line up'. When the wind blows Downstream Do a Double Spey and use the Downstream hand.

The Snake Roll

The Snake Roll is one of the newest casts on the fishing scene – seen by few, and used by virtually none. It has remained a relative secret, and yet it is one of the most useful casts ever developed. It is similar in principle to the Speys, though far easier to learn.

Like the aforementioned Spey casts, the Snake Roll began its life because of a need – not a fishing need but an instructional one. For many years, both my father and I have been teaching the Spey cast. The pool we have used for the last fifteen years is wide, deep and slow, and while it is never a problem showing somebody the Single Spey, the slow current means there is a long wait as the line swings round to the 'Dangle'. This was easily rectified by a series of roll casts, working the line slowly round to the Dangle and ready for the next Single Spey. I was, however, convinced that there was an easier and quicker way to work the line round and started experimenting with different types of roll cast and Spey cast. The end result was the Snake Roll, a very fast change of direction cast and ideal for getting the fly back to the Dangle for the next Spey cast.

You may think there is little use for such a

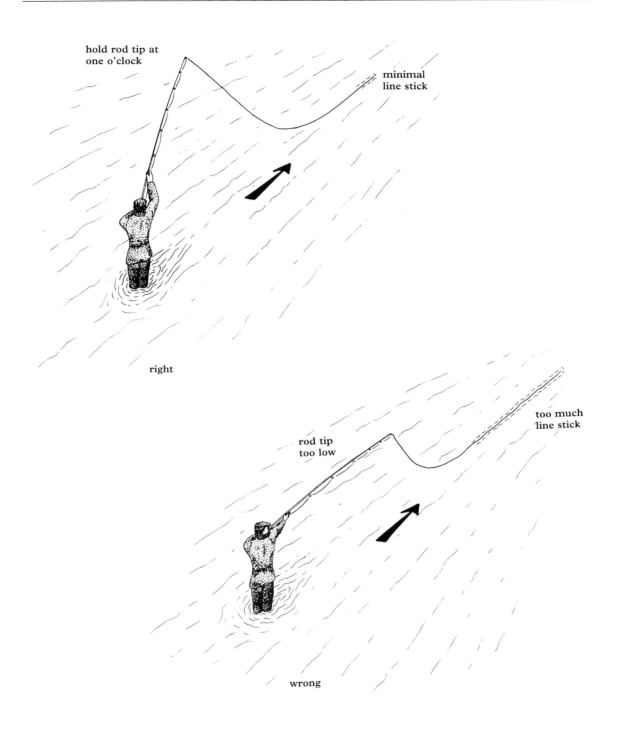

The double Spey cast, stage one.

The double Spey cast, stage two. For angler A, the upstream lead had brought the fly just up to but not across the XY line, denoting the direction of the cast. This will produce the best results. For angler B, however, the upstream lead has been too great and the fly has crossed the XY line. The result of this will be that the forward cast will tangle or cross with the fly line. In all continuous motion casts it is essential *to get the fly and line on the outside of the directional line or, put another way, the directional line must be inside the fly and line.*

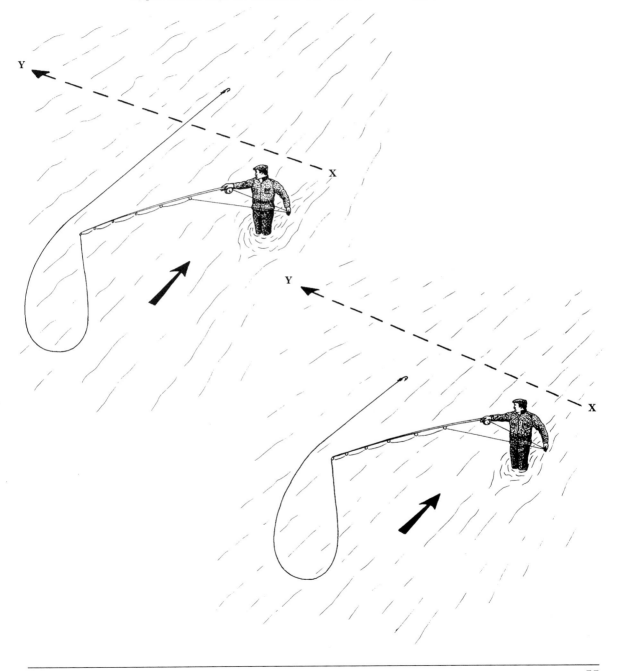

The double Spey cast, stage three. The rod tip must never be dipped (as angler B is doing), as this will stick the line on to the water – the one thing we are trying to avoid. When there is no dip in the rod tip (as with angler A), it describes a horizontal arc.

The double Spey cast, stage four. Make sure you keep the rod tip up, as this lifts the 'belly' and means there is very little stick (angler A). A descending rod tip forces the line down on to the water, increasing line stick along the XY line (angler B).

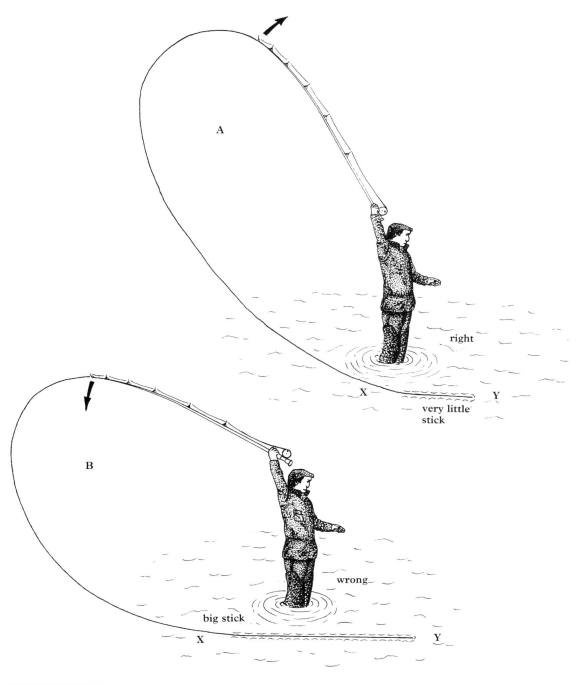

A

right

X   Y

very little
stick

B

wrong

big stick

X   Y

cast. After all, if you have Single Speyed your line across the river, why on earth would you want a cast that puts a fly back on the Dangle? Well, the best use of the Snake Roll is to change direction from left to right – just like the Double Spey in fact. We now teach the Snake Roll as an alternative to the Double Spey because it is three times quicker to change direction and far easier to learn. However, it is not purely confined to the river fly fisher. Stillwater anglers can have enormous success with a cast that changes direction so fast, covering rising fish in an instant. Not only is the Snake Roll faster than an overhead cast, but you can change direction in a single movement. Using an overhead, you need two or three false casts to change the fly's direction.

How do you do it? Start the rod low, level with the water and pointing at the fly. Draw (with the rod tip) one and a half 0s, not from the wrist but from the shoulder. The 0s should be large, quick and in an anti-clockwise direction. Stop the rod tip at one o'clock, watch the line tip hit the water, and then flick the line forward to where you want the fly to go. The most important point to remember with this cast is that you draw your 0 in a plane ninety degrees to where you want the cast to go – easy! It is just as easy to change direction from left to right, though this time you draw your 0 in a clockwise direction, either with the left hand or from the backhand if you are using your backhand.

Like any cast, trying to learn it from a book is rather difficult, but this one is particularly tricky because few others know about it and so cannot tell you where you are going wrong. If you try the Snake and master it, you will find that you catch a lot more fish than before. Not only that, but you will be able to change direction quickly and even fish in situations that you have never even thought about. It usually takes ten minutes to teach someone the Snake Roll, and I think most anglers could teach themselves within half an hour.

Most fly fishers are perhaps aware of five principal casts – the overhead, the roll, the side cast, the Single Spey and the Double Spey – and perhaps the Snake Roll as well. These five or six casts serve most fishing situations around eighty per cent of the time and enable anglers to fish a great variety of water. However, there are plenty of times when none of these casts will get the fly to the fish, and something else is needed.

Heineken Casts

This is where I call for my Heineken (as in the lager) casts. This is a range of casts that has been adapted to suit particular fishing requirements or – to put it another way – Heineken casts reach the fish other casts cannot! There is an enormous number of these casts, each one serving a particular purpose. In fact, I've never had the time to sit down and work out how many Heineken casts there are, but once I did get as far as seventy: thirty-five from the forehand and thirty-five from the backhand!

The simplest way to look at them is to divide them into groups, and this I have done in the following list. As you will see, many of these casts are not really possible with a two-handed salmon rod, though some reading that the Spey casts are involved will probably think they are intended for salmon anglers alone. As I have mentioned before, the Spey casts are not confined to the salmon angler, and any river fly fisher will benefit from these casts, especially those fishing the smaller Devon and Cornish rivers.

Each cast is an extension of an ordinary one, such as the Single Spey. The original name for this type of casting is 'cast stringing', and that is exactly what you are doing – stringing together two or three casts to create a new one. It may be difficult to work out when to use such a cast or perhaps even what some of the terms mean, so I shall run through one to give you an idea.

Let's take the Turbo Single Spey with side cut and Aerial mend. This meets a fairly common situation, particularly on the rivers in the West Country. The angler is fishing from the left bank of the river, wading out about ten feet from the bank behind. The pool is about twenty yards wide with a fast current down the middle, and the lie is under an overhanging tree on the far bank. Normally, the overhanging tree would indicate the use of a side cast, but this is not possible because of

Roll cast and side cut
Single Spey with side cut and shepherd's crook
Single Spey and side cut
Single Spey with Aerial mend
Single Spey with Parachute cast
Single Spey with side cut and Aerial mend
Turbo Single Spey
Turbo Single Spey with side cut
Turbo Single Spey with side cut and shepherd's crook
Turbo Single Spey with Aerial mend
Turbo Single Spey with side cut and Aerial mend
Turbo Single Spey with Parachute cast

Snake Roll and side cut
Snake Roll with side cut and shepherd's crook
Snake Roll with Aerial mend
Snake Roll with Parachute cast
Snake Roll with side cut and Aerial mend
Turbo Snake Roll
Turbo Snake Roll with side cut
Turbo Snake Roll with side cut and shepherd's crook
Turbo Snake Roll with Aerial mend
Turbo Snake Roll with side cut and Aerial mend
Turbo Snake Roll with Parachute cast

Double Spey and side cut
Double Spey with side cut and shepherd's crook
Double Spey with Aerial mend
Double Spey with Parachute cast
Double Spey with side cut and Aerial mend
Turbo Double Spey
Turbo Double Spey with side cut
Turbo Double Spey with side cut and shepherd's crook
Turbo Double Spey with Aerial mend
Turbo Double Spey with Parachute cast
Turbo Double Spey with side cut and Aerial mend

Working out a difficult cast between trees and rocks.

the proximity of the bushes behind. The cast is, therefore, 'strung' from a Single Spey (to change direction), a Double Haul (what we call the Turbo, to get the distance), a side cast (to get under the tree) and an Aerial mend (to stop the fly from dragging or skating on the water).

This pattern is the same for all the Heineken casts. All you need to do is work out which casts are needed to get the fly to the fish, and then string them together. It should work most times, but there are certain casts that cannot be put together – the overhead and side cast, for example, or the Aerial mend and shepherd's crook.

Remember, to be a very good fly fisher you need to be a very good caster and be able to reach the fish that no other angler can get to. With a little thought, some tuition and plenty of practice, you should be able to master the art of cast stringing, and you will then truly be a master caster.

Well, what do you make of all that? I know in my case I certainly need tuition, practice, more skill than I have got and probably a good deal more brainpower as well! Following this piece from Simon, I actually took a fly rod down to my local river, the Bure, after a trout or two. I deliberately chose one of the most difficult sections and had a good mess about, being even more unconventional as usual. I began to see what Simon means and realized unwittingly I was in actual fact making some progress towards the Heineken state of the art that he describes. I think perhaps I have been stringing different casts together to produce something like an end result for a long time now. I stress, however, that what I do is not really done with thought or elegance, and a lot of it is muddled. These words from Simon will certainly make me think a lot more coherently about what I am doing in the future.

3 WHERE, WHEN AND HOW

SALMON FROM SCOTTISH SPATE RIVERS

The Garry

Most of my salmon fishing on spate rivers has taken place on the Moriston and the Garry. The Garry, above Invergarry, was one of Scotland's prime waters back in Victorian and Edwardian times, and even today it is easy to see why. It is glorious to look at, surging through splendid countryside, offering deep swirling pools and the most enticing glides. A hundred years ago the Garry seemed to offer absolutely everything any salmon fisher could ever want, and the catches have been recorded in history.

Today, things are not quite the same. Garry salmon stocks have suffered like those of every other river, but in addition the hydro-electric schemes through the valley have affected salmon runs dramatically. Loch Garry is dammed for hydro-electric power, and fish have to be lifted from the lower Garry into the loch to make their way along the upper river by a type of electronic fish ladder. There is frequent, sometimes fiery debate along the glen as to whether enough fish are actually being allowed through. There are concerns that some are left there over long and so lose their freshness and willingness to travel. Thus, in many ways, the salmon fishing of the upper Garry is not quite what it once was. Even at the head of this river there is another hydro scheme, on Quoich, which has led to a restriction in spawning grounds for those fish that do make their final journey.

Despite all these problems, the upper Garry is a wonderful place to fish, and at certain times of the year there are salmon in numbers great enough to make fishing for them a feasible and profitable occupation. I love it there, even though I know next to nothing about the river compared with the gillies and men from the glen who have grown up along its banks. It is one thing to go into the Tomdoun Hotel, for example, and look at the map of the river there on the wall and see all the named pools, but it is quite another to know the river properly.

There is one man, Farquar, who is like magic on the river. He spends most of the year in Australia, but he returns to the glen every season to lead stalking in the hills that he has known since infancy. However, it's as a fisherman that I know him, and even though he has limited time on the river, you can bet your last dram that he will catch more salmon out of the Garry than all of the rest of the rods put together! Farquar feels for the river just as he does for the hills, and I have known men watch him from high up in the birch woods. He fishes runs where they would never dream of attempting, and they laugh behind their binoculars. Then he catches salmon – often two or three of them – and in silent fury, they mark the spot down. There is no point, though: if there were salmon there, Farquar will have caught them and be on his way!

Still, every now and again, even characters like me are lucky enough to catch a salmon from the Garry. How? By and large (and we are talking about the upper Garry now) the salmon begin to run from the middle of the summer. These first fish are often smaller grilse, but bigger fish do come up with them. They can be in excellent condition and present

Some major Scottish waters: (1) Loch Hope; (2) the Halladale; (3) the Thurso; (4) the Helmsdale; (5) the Brora; (6) Loch Shin; (7) the Cassley; (8) the Oykel; (9) the Carron; (10) the Alness; (11) the Conon; (12) the Beauly; (13) the Ness; (14) the Spey; (15) the Deveron; (16) the Don; (17) the Dee; (18) the north Esk; (19) the south Esk; (20) the Tay; (21) the Tweed; (22) the Till; (23) the Esk; (24) the Annan; (25) the Nirth; (26) the Cree; (27) the Stinchar; (28) the Girvan; (29) the Doon; (30) the Ayr; (31) the Croe; (32) Loch Ewe and Loch Maree; (33) the Kirkraig.

in some numbers; generally, however, there are just a few pioneers that nose their way into the upper river. Catching them can be largely a question of faith.

I remember being up there once in early August making a film on ferox trout for American TV. To catch a ferox trout from that particular area can take a lifetime, and the producer evidently was not about to make that commitment. At the end of a fairly fishless, fruitless week he called me into a meeting, went quite berserk and demanded that I catch a fish of reasonable size for the cameras. I said I'd always made it clear that catching a ferox could be difficult, but my words met a torrent of abuse.

I chose a pool that had not been salmon fished all season and began to work steadily along it with the fly. The camera crew waited and watched, tense, fingers crossed and praying hard! Nothing happened. I then worked along with a spinner. Nothing happened. It seemed as though the whole enterprise was doomed. The director pleaded with me to try again, and the producer paced up and down like some angry Napoleon above us. Then, quite amazingly, out of the corner of my eye I thought I saw a gleam in the water, right on the lip of the pool where the water tumbled down into rapids. I hardly dared hope, but I cast all the same and within minutes found myself netting a beautiful, fresh-run grilse! The day, the film and my reputation were saved.

Choosing a Pool

I tell this story principally to show just how tenuous success can be on rivers like this and how vital it is to watch for every single sign. Also, obviously, the very lip of these pools has always produced the most fish for me. I have already cited the bottom of Loch Poulary itself. Poulary is a beautiful water of some two or three hundred acres, and at times has salmon running all through it. However, it is that particular glide where Poulary empties into a quarter of a mile of rapid that is generally the most

productive area of all. You cannot cast to the salmon that lie there; it is simply too far for either fly or spinner. A boat is necessary, and you have to row very, very gently out into the loch, ship the oars, drift as quietly as possible to within a hundred yards or so of the tail of the loch and then slide out the anchor. The trick is to bring the fly or the spinner round, as enticingly as possible, in front of the fish as they lie and rest, exhausted after their journey up the rapids. It is worth trying this spot virtually every morning because new fish will have moved in during the night, especially from late August onwards when the fish are really beginning to run.

Obviously, all the pools are well worth trying hard, and – after rain especially – from July onwards you can really hope that there will be fish about to be caught. Most of the upper Garry is perfect fly water, and actually most of the biggest fish do fall to fly, very often surprisingly small ones. It is a strange water to fish in many ways because a lot of the pools are so small and intimate that you can fish them quite easily from the bank with a trout or sea trout rod, and double-handed gear is really necessary. Then again, the really big pools, like Horseshoe, are so large that you need one of the hotel boats to cover them adequately.

Farquar's approach is the key to a great many of the salmon successes on the upper Garry in this day and age. Joy Hurst's first fish from the river is a perfect example. We had been fishing a well-known pool for some time with no hint of success when Joy decided to wander above the pool into shallow broken water and try her luck there. One particular place caught her attention, where the river divided behind a rock no bigger than a football. Still, it did create a feature in the water, and she tried a couple of casts both above and beneath it. The second cast beneath found a nice fish of around eight pounds, which took at once. Later, when we tried to explain where the area was, people were amazed. Nobody had had a fish from there for years – if ever.

It is this type of approach that works so well

Beautiful Scottish fly water, but notice the fish ladder behind – testimony to yet another hydro-electric scheme.

on such rivers and you simply cannot afford to leave any water untried and undiscovered. Another example is the area of river below the Tomdoun Hotel, which is dotted with small islands. Very few people fish anything but the main channel, but salmon do not always use this and prefer the areas that go totally unfished year after year. A boat is necessary, but the effort is frequently well worthwhile.

The Burns

Heavy rain is obviously a major key to these spate rivers, and the upper Garry is no exception. Very often late September, for example, sees day-long storms, and the river rises dramatically, which really gets fish on the move. The favourite areas now are the mouths of burns that have become mini-rivers in themselves. The salmon gather at the foot of the burns, even moving a few yards upstream, in ever-increasing numbers, and if the water is still clear enough they will certainly fall to the fly.

These are really wild rivers with no salmon huts, no well-worn tracks, little room for vehicles by the bank and probably no gillies either. It is easy to feel quite alone, but in some ways that is the real joy of it all. The thing to do is to travel light, keep on the move and try and work as much of the river as possible through the course of the day. Success is all about optimism and the belief that every cast will be the successful one. When you are at last successful, you know it is down to you alone, and that nobody has put the fish on the hook for you in any way at all.

THE EARLY FLY FISHER

Tony Jones is an expert salmon angler, who has

In weather like this, it takes a brave man to go out with the fly rod, but often the day will be productive.

caught so many salmon now that numbers in themselves are not the important thing. He would rather just catch salmon in the way that pleases him most. Therefore, he is the perfect man to approach to discuss fly fishing for salmon in the early part of the season when the weather and the water can both be bitingly cold and many of us would rather fish a spinner or bait.

Tackle and Fly

Tony always starts with the fly, providing the water is to some extent on his side. Generally, he begins on the Wye. It is obviously a serious river, and if it is in heavy flood then the fly really is a non-starter. Equally if there is really raw water coming down from its Welsh origins, then the fly will struggle, but Tony believes that salmon will always take the fly if he can get it to the fish and it can be seen at all. A boat can

be useful on a large water like the Wye because it enables you to get the fly right into the best lies. (It is interesting to note that Pashley generally fished from a boat but this was largely because he suffered so badly from arthritis, and he himself maintained that he preferred to fish from the bank when he could.)

Tony generally recommends a medium sink double taper fly line to his pupils and guests. The fast sink is not often used but can play its part occasionally in very deep dark pools where the fish really are lying doggo. Tony is a great believer in the tackle matching the angler, and his views on rod length sum up his philosophy. Many anglers over-rod themselves, and it is easy to lose control of a heavy fly-line in cold weather when there is a strong wind about. A fourteen- or fifteen-foot rod is about right for a medium to large river, and it makes sense to go shorter if the water allows it. Tony would only recommend an angler to go over fifteen feet to a maximum of sixteen and a half feet if the river demands a great deal of Spey casting.

The fly is all-important when discussing these early fish in cold waters, and Tony believes it is vital to make a big impact on them. Remember they are lying deep and half-frozen, and their reactions are much slower than those of summer fish. Tony uses a two- to three-inch tube fly. The names of particular patterns don't mean a thing to him nowadays: all the talk used to be of Jock Scotts or Hairy Marys, but these ancient rules seem to be nonsense to him now. He is solely concerned with impact, and so he uses flies with bright attention-grabbing colours like hot orange, reds, yellows and blacks. In other words, he favours a big, often heavy fly that really shouts out its presence to the fish.

The essential thing is to fish this attention-demanding fly as deep and as slow as possible to salmon that are not going to chase all over the place for anything or anybody. Tony advises a very slow search of all pools, fishing as deep as possible, covering every inch of likely water. It is at this time of the year that the holding pools are probably at their most useful, and Tony pays most of his attention to these.

Method

It is very common to talk about 'perfect' fly water. You know the sort of stretch that I am talking about – nicely broken, nicely paced, with a nice depth – but this type of run only occurs in an ideal world. On rivers like the Wye, Tony stresses that you can can catch fish on the fly without these ideal runs by concentrating on the pools themselves – even if the pools have unbroken surfaces and seem very off-putting to many fly fishermen.

A large, deep early pool where the salmon lie at up to eighteen feet. A pool like this is best fished from a boat.

On the Wye, just as on the Scottish salmon rivers, you can fish an unbroken pool by 'backing up' if you wish. You simply start fishing at the bottom end of the pool rather than (as is more traditional) at the top. You cast straight across the pool; and then take two or three strides upstream. This moves the line itself, and the push of the current increases the action. The angler then begins to hand-line the fly across; so it is really beginning to move, and – in the cold water especially – attract attention. Obviously, the speed at which you want the fly to travel depends a great deal on water temperatures and conditions. The colder the water is, the slower the hand-lining process.

The essential thing, according to Tony, is always to visualize what the fly is doing and to bear in mind the need to put and keep life in the fly. Salmon will, it has to be admitted, take a fly drifting past acting rather like a dead leaf, but not often, and it is the man who really works with his fly and understands its action who will succeed over and over.

Early fly fishing is for when the water and air temperatures are both under fifty degrees Fahrenheit, and once they rise above that mark and stay there for some time, then the floating line can take the place of the sinker. Generally, on the Wye, Tony reckons this change-over takes place around about mid-April, and from then on right through the season the floating line will be his inevitable choice, married with smaller flies that do not need to make nearly as much impact on dour fish. The water will get warmer and clearer and he will tend to move to black-and-silver patterns. Early and later, Tony rarely uses single hooks, simply because he feels the chances of salmon coming unhooked are all the greater. His first preference is nearly always for tube flies, and in summer conditions these will often be tied with small trebles, say tens or even twelves. These small warm-water flies will be dressed on a $\frac{3}{4}$- or one-inch aluminium tube, and now he will begin to look for the shallower, swifter water, often ignoring the pools that were so useful to him a month or so previously.

Kelts

It is the first, cold, few months of the season when you are most likely to land kelts – those spent salmon that are trying, laboriously to return to the sea after spawning. Few salmon survive these rigours (around five per cent overall in many river systems), but a great many survive into the spring and wait in the pools until floods help them downstream to the sea. Sadly, many kelts are mistaken for fresh, spring fish as they can mend surprisingly quickly. However, it is illegal to kill a kelt, and you should try to be very aware of the difference. If you know that you have caught a kelt, then do not be cross with it; it is not the kelt's fault. It is tragic to see how many kelts are abused by salmon anglers who do not realize that they are brave fish. If they do reach the sea, they will return again and perhaps provide somebody with the most memorable day's fishing of his life. You should return all kelts with compassion. Unhook them in the water, with forceps, so that you do not have to handle them or expose them to the air. You may have to support them and keep them upright for a short while until they regain their strength and kick away.

A kelt will be excessively slim, and you will find that the fish looks elongated, with its head too large for its body. Most kelts have ragged fins, especially the tail and anal fins with which they have stirred the gravel. Look carefully at the vents of the fish. If these look raw or unnaturally wide open, then you can be fairly sure that you have caught a kelt. Kelts have flat or sagging flanks and can be discoloured with blotched areas. You will also find that their teeth tend to be unusually large and sharp. Sometimes, too, the fish will have freshwater maggots in its gills. In short, if one or more of these pointers makes you suspicious, then please return the fish. Killing a kelt is a very sad thing to have on your conscience.

Snow still on the mountain tops.

SANDY'S COLD-WATER SPINNERS

I met him on the Dee, one of those really magnificent gillies who knows everything about his river and has forgotten more than you or I will ever know. Altogether I remember being a little intimidated by him and certainly rather in awe of his very stern ways. I was quite keen to fish the fly, thinking in some way this would impress and convince him I was a serious salmon fisher. He would, however, have nothing of it, even though we were well into April.

You see, the weather was disastrous. The nights were freezing cold, there was constantly snow in the air, and for long periods it actually gathered on the ground and even drifted against the salmon hut. There was a persistent, strong wind from the north-east of all places, and even with the stove on, the hut was miserably cold. The water levels were everywhere – up and down on a daily basis – and the river was as dirty as it could possibly be. Water temperatures, like air temperatures were abysmally low for the time of the year, and sometimes you could hardly see anything for driving snow. This, Sandy informed me very decidedly was not weather for the fly.

The only way forward was with the spoon he said, the whole spoon and nothing but the spoon! What spoons he produced: they were all home-made out of brass, copper or tin, and shaped like huge teaspoons. Most were about three inches long but some were even five or six and went out into the wind like bullets. Sandy spent all his time polishing these spoons when he wasn't actually fishing because – he said – the brighter and flashier they were, the more likely they would be taken.

Fishing a Spoon

At first, I fished these spoons ham-fistedly and was told in no uncertain terms that I was retrieving far too fast. Sandy took the rod from me and gave an impressive demonstration. He cast almost directly across the river, put the rod tip down to the water level and hardly reeled at all, letting the current do all the work. We watched the rod tip: it was bouncing steadily and it was easy to imagine the big, burnished spoon kicking, thudding its way around the pool. I say pool, but in fact it was hardly distinguishable that particular week, so swollen was the river.

Sandy hardly reeled in at all that cast. Only when the river had worked the spoon close to our bank did he begin to retrieve at any speed at all, and then only slowly because he said big fish often lurk close in and will take at this critical moment. Of course, working a spoon so slowly and so deep is bound to be hazardous, and over the next four days I lost something in excess of a score of them. Had they been shop-bought, I would have been getting on for a hundred pounds out of pocket, but as they were home-made, it really didn't matter that much. Herein lies the real secret of the home-made lure: buy a big spoon from a catalogue at around five pounds and you are naturally wary of losing it. However, if you make a dozen or more in a winter's evening, then you will be much more light-hearted about the whole exercise and more willing to let a spoon go down deep and slow where it will really do the business.

Another lesson lingers on from that particular week. One of the members of the party refused to have anything to do with Sandy and

The water is near freezing, but the fish still come to the spinner on this particular day.

his spinners, maintaining that it was not the proper way to fish and above all it was a boring method. Boring? Nothing could be further from the truth. The excitement of feeling a big spoon flutter its deep dark passage is intense – especially when there is a strong draw of a taking fish. The man in question preferred to stay in the fishing hut, eating, drinking and pontificating about the fly. At last, one afternoon, he actually took up the rod and went down to the nearest pool. The rod was a long carbon affair with a heavy sinking line it took some effort to mobilize (remember that I said the wind was pretty ferocious), and our friend got all his balance and timing wrong after only three or four casts. Intolerable strain was put on the rod by a combination of the wind and the line working together, and the thing simply splintered into hundreds of matchsticks. The angler was left holding eighteen inches of cork and no dignity! On the next day, he asked Sandy for a spoon.

The Devon Minnow

Any fly fisherman who thinks that spinning is a mindless occupation really should watch Mike Taylor of The Red Lion at Bredwardine fish his Devon Minnows, and think again. Mike uses the traditional Herefordshire Minnows made of light hazel wood for most of his fishing. The idea is to put weight on the line, which will take the minnow down where it will hover about six inches above the bottom. It is the current that makes it spin and pushes it down to where the salmon are. What the angler does

is guide it tantalizingly across the current. Mike is never quite happy: he is always experimenting with the size, colour and weight of the minnows, always chopping and changing to get that little bit of edge. If the water is slack, then a heavy minnow goes off, and a lighter one comes on; if the water is particularly fast, then a weighted minnow will take its place.

The great thing with the Devon Minnow is that you can really feel it working, throbbing on the rod tip. That is important for confidence, and a confident angler fishes with far greater concentration and success. The Devon can also be worked much more slowly around likely lies than a Toby, for example. You can really search every piece of the river bed, letting the Devon flutter its way gradually back to you.

Mike's favourite colours are green and yellow and brown and gold, but if the water becomes

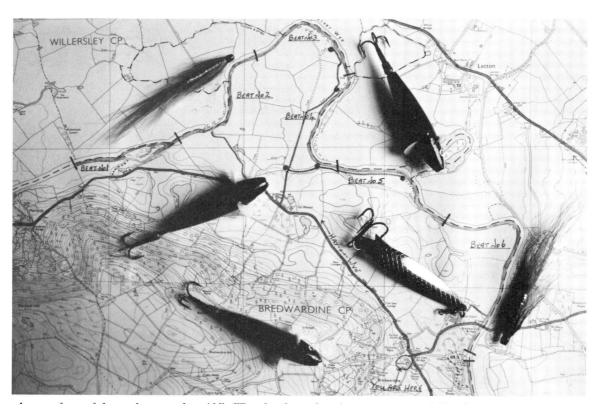

A map of one of the top beats on the middle Wye also shows the minnows, spoons and flies that are the favourites with the local anglers.

Constant concentration is needed for spinning. Notice the gentle arc of the rod.

very cold and clear, then he will move on to a blue and silver. In cold, deep spring water, he will probably be using minnows about three inches long, but as the water warms up two and 2½-inch minnows are more common. In summer, if the river really becomes low, clear and deoxygenated, then he will move on to the tiny one-inch minnows that will still occasionally pick up a fish if used delicately and with imagination.

TROLLING FOR SALMON

Trolling for salmon is a very specialized approach, which is generally restricted to the large lochs through which salmon pass on their way to the rivers and their spawning beds. My own experience of the technique is confined entirely to Loch Ness and to fish that eventually end up in either the Moriston or the Garry rivers. There are those that decry trolling, and certainly it is very far from the so-called sophisticated norm of fly fishing on known pools on attractive rivers. Trolling for salmon is actually a highly skilled, and at times very interesting, way of taking these magnificent fish.

Equipment

Lures

I suppose it would make sense to start with the lures themselves. A vast array is now available, principally imported from America by companies such as the Harris Angling Company. Traditionally, trolling for salmon was carried out with simple spoons or minnows, but there is far more choice. Ideally, the salmon will look

A well-organized troller heads for the best grounds.

for a lure between two and five inches long, one that is quite brightly coloured, works well at speed and does not dive deeper than, say, twelve feet. Many of the lures now available are better for pike or for ferox, both of which tend to feed at greater depths than the salmon. Indeed, talking to many of the Ness trollers, I get the impression most fish seem to come from around six feet, so deep-diving lures and heavily weighted spoons should be avoided.

Rods

Some of the most skilled of the trollers manage to work three, four or even six rods at a time, and so a fair variety of plugs, spoons and spinners can be tried at the same time over a wide area of water. Rod design is not crucial to the troller, but short rods are generally favoured because they are easier to handle in the boat. Of course, you can use a couple of short rods for the close-in lures and longer rods keeping lures further away from the boat and out of tangle range, so a variety of lengths can play quite a part. Poker rods are to be avoided: there needs to be some delicacy and give in the tip, or salmon will be bounced off when they do take. Carbon is the modern material, no doubt, but trolling rods can take a hammering, and often the old glass-fibre rods are a stronger and therefore better bet. It does pay to tie the rod to the boat in periods of windy weather (nearly always in Scotland), or you risk seeing an expensive outfit disappearing forever over the side.

Reels

Reels are probably a more important consideration that the rod itself for the keen troller. The big question is whether to go for a multiplier or a fixed-spool reel, and both types have their champions. For many years, I was ardent in my support of the multiplier, but that was until the bait runner facility appeared on many of the big fixed-spool reels. This allows a fixed-spool reel to be used almost exactly like a multiplier and also gives you the advantages of better, or at least easier, casting and a slightly quicker, less fatiguing retrieve. Whichever you go for, make sure that the spool is big enough to hold a fair amount of line, as there are those trollers that insist you have to work the lures a good way behind the boat – sometimes fifty or more yards.

Line

The line itself is a major issue, and you would be ill-advised to go for anything less than twelve- or fifteen-pound breaking strain for frequently very big fish are involved. Also, trolling takes a great deal out of the line, which can be fatally weakened by twisting or fraying over rocks or other snags. Always inspect your line very carefully, and if you are in any doubt, then change it at once. It is a good idea to change the last ten or fifteen yards or so each time out, for it is this that takes most of the stress and strain. Cheap line is very rarely a true economy when it comes to trolling because it tends to twist faster and so become unusable early on in its life. It would be far better to invest in one of the top brands and use it carefully over many trips. Take care with the line and incorporate swivels on any revolving lure to avoid as much twist as possible. Anti-kink devices are also a very good idea and can save pounds.

Rod Rests

Boat rod rests are a very important issue indeed, and for many years the troller had to make his own. Now, fortunately, there is an increasing number of designs imported from America, and many of them do the job very well. The Harris Angling Company stocks at least one excellent make. The important thing is that the rod rest should grip both boat and rod securely all the time, under any circumstances. A badly designed boat rod rest is a true headache, and it is well worthwhile spending a fair bit of money on this most vital of troller's tools.

Locating the Fish

You are out on the loch probably unsure where to head for. A loch like Ness is simply vast, and you are naturally bemused when you first start. Men who have been trolling Ness and other such lochs all their lives obviously get to know the salmon taking areas over the years and are the experts to consult – presuming they will give up their hard-earned knowledge. Remember, the salmon 'flight paths' are hard won, and you cannot expect people to give them up on a whim. As a general rule, the areas to concentrate on are those close to river entrances into the loch. It is around these areas that salmon are bound to congregate, waiting to make their runs upstream. There is, of course, far more to location than finding the river mouth, but it is a good starting point, and providing you troll fairly quickly, as the salmon in fact likes it, then you should be able to cover a fair bit of water in a single day and perhaps even begin to build up pictures of your own in a week or so.

The modern electronic fish finders (again from America) are an invaluable tool on such big waters. Some people reject them as unsporting, even immoral machines, but that is nonsense in these days of modern high-technology. The fish finders certainly never put fish on the hooks and all they do is give a very valuable insight into what is going on underneath the water surface. Fish finders chart drop-offs, snags and any other features that could attract a group of salmon. They will also record salmon under your boat if you are very, very lucky but the fish tend to move out of the way before they register on the screen. However, if the recorder begins to show large fish underneath you at six or ten feet down then you

A shot of Loch Ness, a famous trolling water.

can be pretty confident that you are covering salmon for pike or big trout tend to hang at twenty feet or deeper.

Fish locators like this can often be hired from the big tackle shops. These tend to be in the south of England, but you can take the finder north with you. Ten pounds a day is a normal rental fee, though deals can generally be done, especially in April or May, which is the coarse fishing close-season so the machines are not likely to be in great demand. Alternatively, two or three friends can club together to buy a machine that will probably cost somewhere around £250. One vital thing about fish locators is that they tend to take any element of boredom out of a day spent afloat. What the screen tells you is invariably fascinating, and you come in quite exhilarated, absorbed by what you have learnt from a vast, seemingly inhospitable stretch of water. Fish locators really are the key to understanding big waters.

Safety Precautions

Never, ever take a loch like Ness, or Mask in Ireland, for granted. Winds can rise alarmingly quickly even on a calm day, and boats do capsize each year with loss of life. Always, therefore, wear buoyancy aids, no matter how calm or settled the day appears to be. If it is a rough day anyway, then map out points or islands that will give you much needed respite from the wind should it rise intolerably. Also, remember that it is far easier to troll with the wind than against it. Even the most experienced troller can run into problems if he is trying to motor into the wind with several baits out – especially if he is out alone.

Unless you are very experienced, it is as well to take the rods in during the battle. Otherwise, you may find a big salmon can wrap every single lure round itself like a parcel and even foul the engine itself. The ensuing tangles can be dangerous as well as frustrating and often the fish itself will be lost.

A fish recorder is an excellent innovation and gives all manner of clues to the patrol routes through the loch.

Salmon will take small trolled deadbaits, but make sure that it is a small trout and not a parr, or even better a dead sea fish.

I tend to strike into the fish, let it run against a reasonably light clutch and reel the other rods in as quickly as possible. This manoeuvre takes about a minute, and the salmon is almost always still on the end. The fight can then be conducted in comparative safety. It is best to put the engine into neutral during the fight: if you need to follow the fish then it is a simple matter to slip into gear and move slowly in the right direction.

Often the troller takes some very big fish indeed, and you have to treat every one with great respect. Even the biggest fish does not always show its colours at once, and I well remember one that came right into the boat so lamb-like that my companion thought it was a trout! He told me there was no need to reel in the other rods and he wasn't even bothering with the net, when suddenly, from the depths, a fish of over twenty pounds soared out of the water. It was a wonderful, if shocking, sight, and we were lucky to get the fish aboard.

In short, never underestimate the skill of the men from Invernessshire, for example, who troll the big, wild Scottish lochs for their salmon. It might not be your ideal picture of salmon fishing, but they are successful through experience, dedication and their own particular brand of skill. This is a method of catching salmon that you would be wise to try before dismissing it entirely out of hand.

FLY FISHING – THE LIGHT APPROACH

Traditionally salmon fly fishing was about anything but the light approach. Robin Armstrong is an angling historian of note as well as one of our best-loved fishing artists. He observes:

The Victorians tended to use [rods] between fifteen and more commonly twenty feet long. They were hideously heavy things weighing as much as three pounds and made up of greenheart with often a whalebone tip. Hickory and lancewood were also frequently used. The rods were expensive because they were true works of art, often with engraved silver butt-caps and carved ivory for the ferrule stops.

They had to be robust for several reasons. Firstly imagine casting those hideous gut-eyed iron hooks of theirs that were like grappling irons almost. And then there was the line itself – straight and level if you were lucky but very frequently uneven so that it would have great difficulty running through the rings. In fact, if you ask me, the line could never be aerialized at all. I haven't seen films of the Victorians casting but I suspect they used a very naive type of Spey cast or a roll cast. You know, they would really whip the fly around the water and never really give it much of an airing at all. To make things worse the rods would almost certainly have drop rings until the 1860s so the line wouldn't fly through those at all anyway. None of this really mattered that much anyway because the Victorians tended to fish just the holding pools and most often from boats so that long casting wasn't particularly important nor was wading or searching out little pockets of water. Obviously given the rivers and the numbers of salmon in them their methods worked very well and from the records we know a hell of a lot of salmon were caught.

The Move to Lighter Tackle

This is much how things were until the 1920s and 1930s, but then A. H. E. Wood came along and turned the salmon world 'topsy-turvy'.

In 1926, Wood's successes were reinforced by the Hardy brothers, who designed a rod to his own specifications. The catalogue said, 'The twelve-foot rod was designed with the assistance of Mr Wood for his particular and successful style of salmon fishing. One of the chief objects was to make a twelve-foot rod feel lighter in the hand and not be so tiring to the wrist and yet retain all the power necessary for long casting and handling of a heavy fish'.

Twelve feet! It was a far cry from the rods of fifty years before and a move towards the type of salmon fly fishing now practised on our smaller spate rivers. The impetus was not purely British, and we have a great deal to thank the Americans for, because they pushed ahead with the concept of using single-handed rods – often only seven or eight feet in length – and light floating lines. To some extent their approach could afford to be different because their rivers are often more lively, more filled with oxygen, and their fish are more active. Richard Gibbs takes this latter point up when he explains the basics of fishing in Labrador and Newfoundland to his guests.

Richard is at real pains to stress that the long rods, heavy lines and methodical casting so very common on our classic rivers do not really work when transported across the Atlantic. He describes the approach as an 'on your toes' type of fishing. The idea is that you fish light, are prepared to wade as much as possible, don't just fish the bigger pools, are constantly experimenting and, above all, fishing with the mind as much as with the body. Every piece of water calls for a different approach and demands that the fly be fished at varying depths, speeds and distances. He is quite adamant that those who catch the most fish are those who work the hardest, think the most and use light gear that is in total harmony with the job in hand.

The Gordon Heath Approach

There can be little doubt that this approach

Gordon Heath with a superb salmon, caught on little more than trout tackle.

works exceptionally well, especially on the smaller spate rivers. Gordon Heath is an extraordinary man – a Welshman now living in Scotland and running one of its most appealing fishing hotels. Gordon has brought many of his Welsh habits with him, and it is an education to walk down the river, watching him fish. The first thing one notices is that he only uses trout tackle, with a heavier leader than you would expect. Six or seven pounds is the general run. Unless the water is particularly murky, from April or May onwards he also uses flies that many would consider exceptionally small – twelves and even sometimes fourteens.

Of course, Gordon does head to the known pools and runs, and he whisks through those

first, but quickly so that he can move on and investigate all the little pockets up and down the river that most of us never even consider. There is absolutely nothing conventional or stylized about Gordon's approach. He works his fly at very different speeds through the various bits of water. Sometimes he will mend the line frequently so the fly moves at the pace of the current; at other times he will allow a belly to form in the line so that the current builds up and pushes the fly through considerably faster than the water speed; sometimes, especially on narrower necks of water, he will simply lean out and let the fly dibble in the current, quite high and near the surface. Often he uses a combination of all three techniques so the fly is put over fish at constantly differing rates.

The moral that both Richard and Gordon preach, therefore, is to break conventional modes of thought, to use trout tackle (at least heavy trout tackle) and approach every yard of water with an open mind. There are those who learn to Spey cast beautifully, like machines, and the physical pleasure of delivering the line, rhythmically, superbly, over and over at the same pace at the same distance is almost enough for them. However, hardly surprisingly, it is not always these men who catch the most fish. It is more often somebody like Gordon, totally non-textbook, perhaps not elegant to watch but not afraid to put any idea into practice.

FLOODS ON EXMOOR

Late one month a depression began to sweep in from the Atlantic. The clear sky faltered into mist trails and then heavy cloud. Temperatures dropped, the wind rose and it began to rain hard cold drops all over Exmoor. It rained all day, through the night and well into the following day. Two inches fell in all, and the Barle began to rise and colour and thunder off the moor to swell the waters of the Exe itself. It was a fine rain that the county had cried out

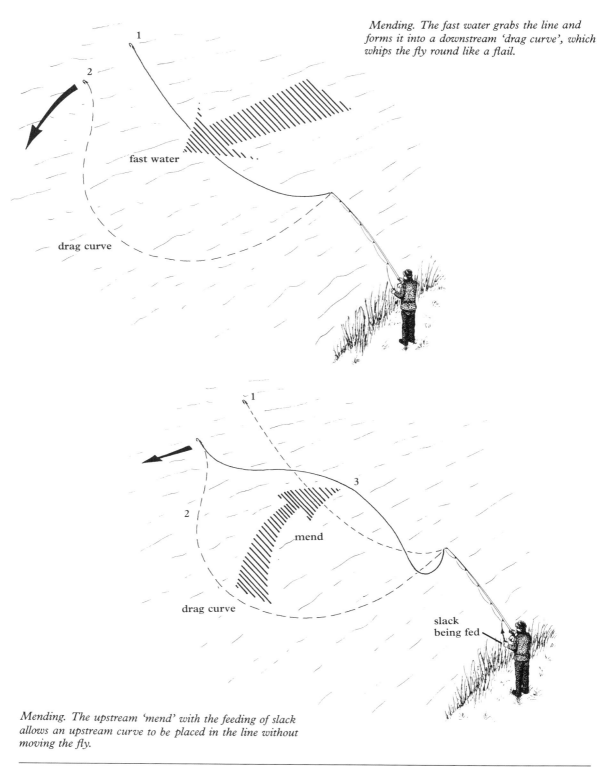

Mending. The fast water grabs the line and forms it into a downstream 'drag curve', which whips the fly round like a flail.

fast water

drag curve

mend

drag curve

slack being fed

Mending. The upstream 'mend' with the feeding of slack allows an upstream curve to be placed in the line without moving the fly.

for. As the waters rose, so the salmon burst into life, flocking up the Exe, pushing into the Barle and filling pools that had been empty virtually all summer long.

Most of these fish were grilse or small salmon between four and twelve pounds, though the average would be around five pounds. I've yet to hear anyone complain about this: these sleek, silver splendid salmon look and fight like rockets and fit their twinkling rivers perfectly, able to slide and squirm right up to the redds as high as Withypool and Simonsbath.

It was Friday, about 3.00 a.m., when the rain began, and by a wishy-washy dawn, the Exe was already rising and colouring, festooned with leaves, weed and branches. The salmon were orgiastic. In one pool, twenty fish were leaping, cartwheeling, rolling – stabbing the feeble daybreak with their light. I was at least as feverish, casting, casting with never a stop, painfully aware that water visibility was dropping each minute and with it my chances. Then there were two tugs and a five-pounder that leapt high and was off. That made up my morning.

By 10.00 a.m. the fly was done for totally, and I returned to the Barle, which was rising, looking lovely but still without fish. I walked it for hours in the rain, watching, praying, but not until 6.00 p.m. did I find a six-pounder newly arrived in the Vicarage Pool. It was obviously still disorientated, roaming here, flitting there, never still, simply looking for a hole to call home. It saw my fly three times, turned and even followed once, but other things were clearly on its mind. At 7.00 p.m. in a premature gloom I squelched back to the fire at the Tarr Steps.

'Leave them till Monday', was all the advice, but I couldn't. I was leaving in twenty-four hours, so I spent one of those uneasy nights enjoying the warmth, good food and company, fearful for the next day, listening to the rain down the gutters.

A damp dawn and hope bubbled as I walked to the river, but the water was above the steps of the ancient clapper bridge, and the pool of the previous night was lost in the surge of

Within its banks this time!

brown. I decided to fish until breakfast, but I knew that I was done for on the Barle.

I packed and paid, and poddled down the valley, through grey Hawkridge and drab Dulverton. Then a miracle happened. Under the old town bridge the Exe ran high, coloured, but just about fishable, and within fifteen minutes that was exactly what I was doing. I caught my salmon within some thirty minutes of beginning. It was a bright seven-pounder and I decided to take it because I had worked so hard, because it was a cock and because there seemed plenty of fish in the river and I knew it would be my last. The Exe now was rising, looking more and more like the pre-breakfast Barle, and I knew I had been a very lucky man indeed.

This is a story told simply to highlight the

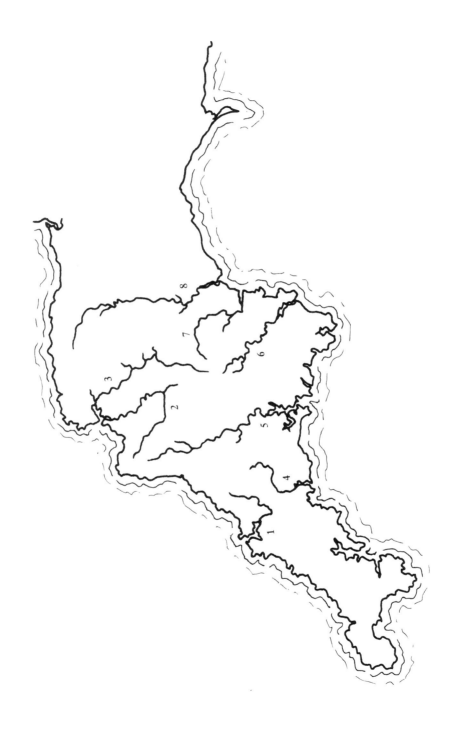

Some major rivers of the south west: (1) the Camel; (2) the Torridge; (3) the Taw; (4) the Fowey; (5) the Tamar; (6) the Dart; (7) the Teign; (8) the Exe.

eccentricities of these short, small spate rivers that can be up and down as fast as a fiddler's elbow and take a lifetime's experience to even guess at predicting.

THE STREAMS OF THE SOUTH-WEST

Even though waters like the Barle and the Exe are known as rivers, they are little more than streams in comparison with the Tay or the Tweed. They are often only five yards across with the tiniest of pools – barely as long as the salmon itself. It is essential to be flexible – the removed, rather impersonal approach that can be used on the big rivers is totally out of place here, and to succeed you really have to make yourself as one with the stream.

Above all, you have to use your eyes and travel the river very, very carefully indeed not risking a single false footstep and not overlooking the tiniest piece of water. You have to believe that if salmon are up, then they can and often will be anywhere in the river, and that includes being pressed against the bank beneath your very feet.

Polaroid glasses are an absolute must on this type of stream, for they offer the most perfect opportunities to cast to salmon that you can actually see. This is not only the most exciting form of salmon fishing there is, it is also a tremendous boon for the angler: you can see the fly, its course and the salmon's reaction, and make amendments that are necessary. This is really live-wire fishing – all about identifying with the river and tuning in with its salmon stocks as closely as is humanly possible. Hope, I believe, is the most important ingredient when fishing these waters. You have got to believe that there are fish present virtually everywhere in the river! By that I mean you must take the time to check every possible shake or shimmer that you see in the water. Remember that a salmon can lie nearly invisible in six inches of water, but if you spook him, you've lost him for the day if not for good.

I get a surge of adrenalin, mixed with a twinge of smugness that my stalking has been successful, every time I see a salmon like this – that is until I think of how many fish I must have disturbed unwittingly and begin to worry that that fish that I have seen has seen me too. Nothing can be taken for granted on such waters. Once a fish is sighted, I simply freeze, melt into cover as best I may and weigh up the challenge.

It is as well to work on the assumption that you will only get a single chance and that you have got to make the very most of it. Therefore, you must work out exactly where you have to place the fly for it to swim at the right level and at the right distance from the fish. It is worth spending a good deal of time watching the water speed and looking for any change in the current's direction that you can use or which could work against you. I also take time to look carefully at all the surrounding water. How will I make my approach to a casting position? On which rocks shall I stand? are there any snags that will catch on the back-cast or in the water itself? Then I even think about playing the fish. Are there any obvious dangers to keep a fish from in those initial rushes? Where will I steer it at the end of the battle when I am looking for quiet water?

Finally I will check the fly itself. I make sure that I am totally happy with the pattern, that the point is sharp, that the fly sinks true, that all the knots are secure and that the hook length has not frayed on the rocks in the river. I will probably let the fly fall in the water at my feet a couple of times just to make sure that air has not been trapped in the dressing, and then at last I know I am ready. This type of concentration is good for me, I know, for it breeds a mental calmness and helps control the pounding of my heart. Then it is a question of choosing every foothold so that nothing breaks and I send out hardly a ripple or a vibration. All this physical and mental energy subdues unruly passions, and I creep out into the river, knowing that I will do my very best with the opportunity that has been presented.

Carrying a lovely grilse to the bank.

In this situation, the best that you can hope for is that the salmon sees the fly, smacks into it and is hooked almost before either of you knows it. More likely, the fish will see the fly, begin to shift its position and perhaps take the fly lightly in its jaws. A delayed strike can be successful if you keep calm and give just a little slack. So far, so good, but what about the fish that rolls over the fly, comes short or simply nips the tail feathers? Perhaps then it is best to cast again at once, hoping the salmon will be agitated and snatch it in earnest once it is given a second chance. If that fails, I retire back into the undergrowth, watch the fish carefully and try it in five or ten minutes with another fly. Should that approach draw a blank too, then all I can do is mark the fish's lie exactly and try him on the way back home, perhaps in a

few hours, when he may be more obliging.

I do not believe that you can put a fly to these small stream salmon too accurately or with too perfect a presentation. To do that obviously takes some casting skill, but you've also got to think about your approach to the water and position yourself to the best possible advantage. To do this, very frequently, you need chest waders or at the very least good thigh boots. Over and over, I've been caught out when wearing wellingtons alone. I simply haven't been able to position myself to put in a really telling cast, and nothing is more frustrating.

Equipment

For the rest, I prefer a single-handed ten- or eleven-foot trout rod, much the same as anybody would use on a stillwater reservoir. The line, obviously, should be matched to the rod but a Number 8 is about right. As far as I am concerned, the line must float. A floating line, you see, I find much easier to control, to lift off the water carefully and without disturbance so that the fly itself might move enticingly upwards towards the surface. With a floating line you can mend any loops that the current produces and drift a fly yards downstream. A sunken line can easily get trapped on underwater rocks or round sunken branches and is not nearly as easy to lift over approaching snags. My own whim is for a slightly darker-coloured floating line than the normal white or yellows. (This is probably not founded in any facts at all, but only because on half a dozen occasions a salmon has actually risen at the line itself when I have used white. This has never happened when I moved to a darker shade of green.) The nylon cast, I am not actually too concerned about. My own feeling is that the point should be eight- or ten-pound breaking strain minimum: I don't believe that the diameter of the line puts fish off much, and I think it is only fair to make sure that you land whatever fish you hook and not leave it with a fly in its jaws. This advice was given to me by a couple of water bailiffs many years ago when they found me using a five-pound point. They told me there was no reason for it, and since then they have been proved correct on many occasions.

The question of flies is more complex. When the colour of the river is high, I prefer a larger brighter fly, but once the rivers fine down, quickly as they do, then obviously a smaller drabber pattern begins to work its own magic.

Tips from a Local

Patrick Veale now runs that famous old firm of fishing tackle dealers in Dulverton, Lance Nicholson. No one knows the rivers of the area better than he, and here are his views of fly choice particularly.

The rivers we mainly cover are the Exe,

including the Barle, Taw, Torridge and East Lynn. The Exe system produces the most fish. Depending on the water, the small run of spring fish will enter the river in March, while the main Autumn run comes from July to the end of the season in September. The Exe and Barle seem to like a bit of yellow in the flies and Stoat's Tail, Yellow Garry Dog, Yellow Torrish and Munro Killer are all very popular. The GP prawn and shrimp flies also catch their fair share of fish on these rivers.

The Taw and the Torridge are dirtier rivers than those of the Exe system because they run through agricultural land and take a fair amount of run-off whenever it rains. These rivers begin in March, and several spring fish are usually caught. Also, these rivers have a run of sea trout from June onwards, which the Exe for some reason does not have. These rivers are fly-only, after 1 May. Orange seems to be very attractive throughout these rivers: the Munro Killer, the

This slim fish is returned to forge upstream to his final destiny.

Stoat's and Orange, Thunder and Lightning, Willie Gunn, Stoat's Tail, the GP prawn and the shrimp flies are all favourites. The early season sees a lot of people using large Waddingtons, while later on, when the water drops, trebles and even smaller flies on double hooks are used more commonly.

The East Lynn is a very difficult river to fly fish, but those that do persevere often use the Hairy Mary, the Teal Blue and Silver and frequently a Jock Scott. A touch of blue often seems to work wonders on this particular river for some reason.

You will appreciate all this is a brief rule of thumb, but I would be quite happy fishing with these flies alone. However, as is the way with salmon fishing, other flies get used occasionally and are quite successful as well. Many of the flies that I have mentioned are applicable on all the rivers and should do throughout the season. If I had to add anything to the list, I would include the Silver Stoats Tail, the Silver Doctor, the Tosh and occasionally even a Muddler.

It is also worth remembering here that Simon Gawesworth has said that the Spey cast can be very useful on these smaller rivers, even with the single-handed trout rod. There is a tendency to think of the Spey only in conjunction with the traditional salmon rod, but this is not the case. Indeed, when fishing these small often overgrown beats, any cast that gets a fly in the right place should be used, and convention should be the last of considerations.

SALMON OF THE WESSEX RIVERS

Dave Steuart has been fishing for salmon in the Test, Itchen, Avon and Frome for well over quarter of a century and now actually lives on the Test. No man is better equipped to discuss the salmon populations of these rivers than he. According to Dave, the salmon of these cherished waters have declined more viciously than in any other part of Britain, and he sees several deadly reasons for this.

Causes of Decline

First of all, we have to consider the increase of population in England as a whole, and particularly the south, off the M4 corridor. More people have made more demands on the environment, and it is the salmon above all that have suffered.

Let us look first at the demand for cheap water in the region. This has meant that water authorities have begun to abstract water from the top of the rivers. This has led, quite obviously, to a major decline in flow rates and, now, as the rivers are less healthy, they are less able to cope with increased pollution.

Silting

Increased pollution there certainly has been. Look at the developments made in farming in the last quarter of a century, prompted by every financial demand. The increase in chemicals on the land has polluted the rivers. Farmers are also demanding that their fields discharge water more quickly, and drainage dykes have been cleared, dug and straightened all over the region. This means that when it rains everything runs off quicker, washing silt in abundance into once-pure streams. This silt, naturally, sinks and covers the traditional redds of the salmon, and the number of hatching eggs is pitifully decimated. Think too of the alevins that do hatch out: all that suspended silt is too much for them. It clogs up their gills and can lead them to die within days.

The Trout Farms

In addition, the Wessex rivers have seen some of the most gigantic fish farms built in Europe. Indeed, one of those on the Avon produces tens of thousands of rainbow trout each year. Just think of the waste that those fish produce. There is more to production than meets the eye. In fact, the sewage entering the Avon from this one fish farm, Dave has calculated to be the equivalent of what is produced by a town like Romsey. Naturally all these untreated wastes have drastically changed the character of the river's fly life: now there are less of the 'old style' flies, like mayflies, and more of the chironomids – midges and the like. For salmon used to feeding in particular ways in these rivers, such a switch of foodstuffs is naturally undesirable.

Indeed, of all the problems on the Wessex rivers Dave sees the trout farms as the most significant. All sorts of problems are produced. Take, for example, the amount of adult rainbows that appear in the rivers. Are these simply escapees? Dave believes, and there is evidence to back him up on this, that many are actually released on purpose by the fish farm owners. What happens is that fish farmers grow rainbows on until they know how many the market is going to need. Any surplus is simply uneconomic, and the easiest thing is to cut and run, to let them go and to fend for themselves. How do large rainbows fend for themselves? They eat small fish, and of course salmon parr will be at the top of the list.

Chemical Pollution

What goes in must come out, and the increased population of the area has led to a superabundance of human waste. This is treated, unlike the waste from the trout farms, but it still finds its way into the rivers and increases the chemical cocktail that is slowly strangling the rivers.

Twenty years ago, according to Dave, it was quite possible to drink the waters of the Test or the Itchen, but now you would be ill-advised to paddle in them with bare feet. Then, the water was like something that flowed from the tap. It was not just clear: you could count the pebbles at twenty feet, but now all that has changed and with it the salmon populations of these marvellous rivers.

The Impact on the Salmon

Now other factors begin to take control. Consider this. If there are fewer fish running the rivers, those that are caught by anglers represent a far greater percentage of fish that will not reach the redds to spawn. For example, in

1993 – according to Dave – some two hundred salmon were caught in the Test out of around five hundred running the river. We say five hundred, but the counters cannot differentiate between big sea trout and salmon, so the number could have been as low as three hundred. If two hundred salmon were caught and perhaps 150 of those were killed, out of three hundred, potential breeding stock were reduced by fifty per cent by the anglers. It is no wonder that Dave is backing policies of catch and release.

The size and age of the salmon running these rivers has also changed dramatically. Now the majority of fish seen in the rivers are grilse rather than salmon. You see, most salmon need to survive in the rivers from spring to December, when they spawn, and the chance of being caught is correspondingly high. Even greater than this is the danger that salmon face out at sea, now that the netsmen are so active there. A salmon has to exist for three or four years in its saline feeding grounds. However, a grilse only has a year at sea and is more likely to survive and return to its home waters. Certainly, Dave increasingly sees the big Avon and Test springers as something he enjoyed in the past.

The Argument for Catch and Release

Grave as the situation can seem, Dave has not given up – not by a long chalk. At present he is engaged in a research programme into the salmon runs of his local rivers and is releasing every fish that he catches tagged and with a transmitter in its stomach. With these transmitters in place, scientists and fishery workers can follow the fish upriver and see exactly what is happening to them during the remainder of their lives.

This is an encouraging development, and it provides an argument against those who decry catch and release. Their main argument is that fish caught and released will die, but now Dave has positive proof to the contrary. In the 1993 season Dave caught, tagged and released

This scene could not have been imagined even fifteen years ago – a British salmon being returned.

twenty-six fish, and to his certain knowledge at least twenty-four survived (remember that these twenty-four also carried transmitters forced into their stomachs). Indeed, one fish that was tagged and wired for sound was recaught a few weeks later and fought heroically once again. Surely the argument against catch and release has to be abandoned.

Therefore, there is hope, but Dave accepts that the fishing on these rivers is still very expensive, and a man is unlikely to get a season rod for much less than a thousand pounds if the beats are of much worth. Having paid that amount of money, the pressures on him – from his own wallet and probably from his partner – are going to be substantial. It is hard to justify returning a fish when such sums are involved, but it has to be done. There has to be a lot of

goodwill and a lot of honesty if the Wessex rivers are ever going to be returned to their former glory. Honesty? Yes – inasmuch as fishery owners have to admit there has been a deterioration and will have to spend money and effort trying to put things right. The public, too, will have to cooperate, and support organic farming. How excellent, for example, if human waste could be ploughed into the fields like it was centuries ago rather than pumped, chemically treated, into the rivers to do untold damage.

Make no mistake. The salmon stocks of these famous rivers do stand in the balance. Just because the River Test is known throughout the world is no guarantee that salmon will continue to swim there into the next century. Indeed, many of the signs suggest that they will not. Just think how many rivers have lost their populations of fish – not just salmon – and then consider why the Test should be spared alone. The increase in man's numbers around the globe has had horrendous effects wherever we look, and although the valleys of the Test and the Avon are still superficially magnificent, beneath the surface of the rivers there flows a different tale.

FISHING THE PRAWN

Dave Steuart also seemed to be a very good person to discuss fishing the prawn. Use of the prawn is very common indeed on the Wessex rivers and can be a killing method. One excellent thing about Dave is that he is not hidebound in any way by snobbery or old-fashioned ideas. If the prawn works – or anything else – then he will use it. Dave's background is that of a tremendous fisherman for all species, and whether he is after a dace or a salmon, he will pursue it with true efficiency. Dogma plays no part at all.

Tips

He says, laughingly, it doesn't matter if you use one, two or even three trebles, the fish will fall off! That seems to be the biggest problem as far as Dave is concerned when using the prawn – putting the hook into the fish so that it stays there. Nowadays, after many years of experimentation, he is very happy to mount the prawn on a piece of wire which is then attached to the line by a loop. Now – and this is the interesting bit – Dave uses a single size 4 treble, which he hooks through the prawn's head.

The idea is that when the fish takes the prawn, the wire will be blown up the line, leaving a single treble attached. The thinking is just like that involved in the design of a Devon Minnow which, too, leaves the fish's mouth and rises up the line once the battle commences. Obviously, the hope is that the fish does not have a bait to work against and loosen the hookhold. It certainly works for Dave, although there are always some that will come off, especially with the prawn it seems, and nothing is certain about salmon fishing in any way at all.

Dave likes to fish his prawns on paternoster tackle so that the lead is bouncing along the bottom with the prawn a foot or so above. The thinking is that most salmon lie close to the bottom, and that is where you want to fish the prawn. The paternoster keeps it in this killing area and allows it to rise and fall according to the bottom contour. Obviously, the prawn can also fish under a float, but that is not quite so flexible and the prawn is fished at a predetermined level irrespective of the contours.

What other rules are there, according to Dave? Well, he would always take issue with the concept of 'rules', but there are various guide lines. For example, he would use a biggish prawn in the spring and move down to a shrimp or the last two segments of a prawn in the summer – yes, the last two segments. There are a lot of fishermen who are only happy using the entire perfect prawn, but this doesn't seem to matter to Dave at all. In fact, he says, that very many times he will lose the head of a prawn to a chub, but that does not seem to affect the prawn's salmon-taking abilities later on.

It is just the same with the type of prawn: many like to use English prawns because they still have their legs and feelers intact and look a lot better on the hook – to us. Dave is just as happy, however, using Norwegian prawns that are generally trimmed right round. This makes one think that it is the smell of the prawn that is important, and that is probably the case. We all know how acute the salmon's sense of smell is, and there is no doubt that a prawn entering a pool is immediately scented and approached. In all probability, the prawn reminds the salmon of rich feeding days in the ocean, but it's impossible to be quite sure on this.

One point that Dave would argue, however, is the question of salmon and their sight. They cannot be colour blind, for as he says, very

Fishing either the prawn or the worm is not a mechanical job in any way at all: constant vigilance is needed as well as a good idea of what the current is doing and where the fish lie.

frequently one shrimp will be ignored but another of a different colour taken immediately. An assortment of colours can therefore be nothing but a bonus.

Dispelling the Myths

Any discussion with Dave makes you realize that he hates making hard-and-fast statements, and he hates a great deal of the stuff that is written down as gospel. In fact, he believes that whole chapters of rubbish have been carried from one book to another, from one father to his son. This is the case, he believes, with the old belief that the prawn will work when nothing else succeeds. Indeed, Dave fishes the prawn in quite the opposite way and will often run it through a pool before anything else. Why bother trying other methods when you are brimming with confidence in the prawn? The other piece of folklore he disputes is that the

prawn ruins the pool for anybody else following. It doesn't. The prawn can be fished through a pool, over and over, quite fruitlessly, and yet the Mepps, for example, will be taken first cast afterwards. According to Dave, this rumour was spread around by fly fisherman who did not like the thought of the prawn at all.

Dave has seen fish actively frightened by prawns, it is true, but these are almost invariably salmon that have encountered some hostility on their way from the sea – perhaps they were foul-hooked, on purpose or accidentally. There is no doubt in Dave's mind that a fish that has been foul-hooked is terrified if it has managed to get away. It does not matter nearly as much if the fish is hooked in the mouth and breaks free: that salmon will come again at a bait quite readily. It is a quite different thing if a spinner has caught it in the back, the tail or the belly. The brain of the salmon might not be a particularly complex machine, but the difference between the two types of hooking is obviously understood.

Method

If the water is dirty, Dave will tend to fish the prawn in rather more shallow steady runs. Should the river be very clear, he will probably look for his fish in the deep pools, anything between fifteen and eighteen feet. Indeed, on rivers like the Test, he does not like to fish the pools at all when the river is really murky, but instead looks for three feet of water going through with a steady push. Obviously, the salmon need that little bit of light if they are going to feed positively.

Prawn fishing is exciting. There can be no doubt of that at all. If you are fishing the Mepps, all you really feel is a bang, and you're in. Not so the prawn. Very often you will feel it just being nipped. Dave has watched many a fish follow a prawn across a pool and perhaps bang it with its head, mouth closed. However, nine times out of ten, that fish will come again next cast and give a positive take. In fact, Dave has been frequently hailed as a minor god for predicting this very occurrence. He feels that bang on the line on cast one, and confidently says to his fishing partner that he expects to catch a fish the next cast. So it happens, and a legend has been created! (I just hope that I have not destroyed the fun!)

When a fish takes, it is important to let it walk away with the prawn, and Dave tends to let them take a yard or so of line before striking. Then we just hope that treble goes in, and the prawn clears off up the line out of harm's way, and the fish will be landed. If it is fortunate enough to be landed by Dave himself, it is almost certain to be returned, hopefully to get to its spawning bed and fulfil nature's purpose for it.

One thing that filters through from a conversation with Dave is the overwhelming feeling that here is a man who really understands rivers and sees water in a truly three-dimensional way.

This is a real gift for a salmon fisherman, and in Dave's case it has been built up through years of observation as well as fishing the float for roach or dace. Dave understands about the way that currents operate and why salmon lie where and how they do. On rivers like these, it pays to watch the water hawk-eyed and identify the various back-flows, or cross-flows, and those pieces of water where there are two current speeds operating. The salmon, obviously, knows all these different wrinkles in the river intimately and intuitively, and the nearer the prawn fisherman can come to identifying them, the more likely he is to succeed.

WELSH SALMON

Wales is primarily sea trout country, or that at least is the perception we have of it. Throughout Wales, the sea trout is God to the men who live beside the Teifi, the Towey, the Rheidol, the Conway and many, many other rivers, some of which are little bigger than streams. These are the men who are out, night after night, whenever they think the sea trout might be running. They fish on hard-pressed Association waters, where success demands a high skill and a total understanding of the dark waterside. A hero of them all is Cecil Thomas, a man well over seventy years of age and Vice Chairman of the Llandysul Angling Association. He first encountered the beloved sewin on the River Teifi in the 1920s, and in over sixty years he has rarely taken fewer than a hundred fly-caught fish each season. He fishes still, and he will always do so in the dark pools, spreading his lines through the grabbing branches and guiding his fly down to where the big fish lie. Cecil is just one Welsh sewin man, and he represents thousands of others. He also knows a fair bit about salmon in the Principality and here are his comments.

There have been all sorts of changes in Welsh salmon fishing since the War. Some of it is good news, and some of it not so good. Up

Some major Welsh rivers: (1) the Conway; (2) the Clwyd; (3) Dee; (4) the Severn; (5) the Wye; (6) the Usk; (7) the Tawe; (8) the Towy; (9) the Teifi; (10) the Aeron; (11) the Mawddach; (12) the Glaslyn; (13) the Llyfni.

until the 1940s, most if not all the fishing was owned by very rich land owners, and the average man just never got a look in at all. However, the War changed all that sort of thing, and since the 1950s more and more river has been up either for sale or for lease. Mind you, the prices have rocketed, partly because of outside interest. For instance, in the 1950s the Prince Albert Club from Macclesfield started buying up pieces, and that pushed the price up for us in Wales. Anyway, the situation now is that great lengths of water are controlled by Associations with long lists of members who pay very moderate fees indeed. My own club for instance owns twenty-six miles of water and only charges £95 a year. Some would consider that high because it has good runs of salmon and sea trout. If you move further up the rivers, where brown trout are the major species, then you can expect to pay £45 or £50 for the season. The end result is that the average man in Wales can get his salmon fishing much much cheaper than most men can do in Scotland or really anywhere else outside parts of Ireland.

That's the good news; the bad news is that very often, as I have said, the rivers are leased out, often on five-year leases. That always makes it difficult for a club because you don't want to put in time and money improving the banks and the water if you are going to be kicked off. A lot of the rivers need real management, but short leases do not encourage clubs to invest in the future. This is short-sighted, and it really should change for the good of Welsh fishing.

The other thing that has changed is the decline in big spring salmon. This is a tragic shame and the super springer is now a very rare creature indeed, especially since the 1950s and the 1960s. The springer spawn way up the river system, in the really tiny rivers and streams. Over the last thirty years, since agriculture became really intensified, these headwaters have very often become too badly polluted to allow the salmon to spawn successfully. Even if they do spawn, pollution has seen to it that there are no tiny food items living for the parr to feed on. As a result, these headwaters and feeder streams are now very hostile environments for the big spring

I don't know why I was looking so smug – it had been a poor day so far.

salmon, and you can see why this type of fish has been on the decline. On the other hand, research seems to prove that the summer and autumn fish spawn in the middle reaches where the pollution is less intense. You can see, then, that it is these smaller, later-run fish that predominate. Of course, these are highly desirable in themselves and average around about eight pounds with a few twenty-pound fish coming out every year, but it is a shame that the monsters seem to be something of the past.

When to Fish

You've got to realize that the whole key to Welsh salmon fishing is the rain. All the good Welsh salmon waters are spate rivers, and they rise and fall very quickly indeed. Get a good flush of rain, and the river shoots up, and the salmon swarm in. As soon as it stops raining, and the river begins to fall, you have a bonanza. This is the key time, just before the fish are settling back into the pools and becoming dour again. The water is still fairly coloured but dropping fast, and the fish will come to spinner, worm or the fly.

Once the rains have been gone for a while, you begin to struggle, and this is typical of summer fishing. The Welsh rivers almost always have very short pools indeed. There is very little open water that is good and deep, and once the sun begins to shine again, the salmon push into the very deepest water in these enclosed pools. This makes it very difficult indeed to catch salmon regularly on the fly, and for this reason most of the Welsh salmon fishermen who are really serious are wormers. You *can* take them on the fly after a spate or quite frequently in the evening or very early morning. At that time they will come forward in the pool into the white-water, and then you will be able to pick them up from time to time. Not many people fish for salmon with the fly in Wales and there are no real standard patterns. My own particular preference, especially on the Teifi, is the Logie. I fish them tied very small indeed for salmon because the whole skill is fishing quite tight and tight in the half-light.

The real salmon experts, though, are nearly always worm men. Generally, especially after a spate, it's best to use a bunch of three or even four lobworms on a big hook, probably a size 2. The idea is to bounce those worms about and get them searching the entire pool. When the level drops and the water clears and the heat builds up, then you will have to scale down, and very often salmon will be taken on a single worm and much smaller hook. You will find the village children from all over fishing the pool with worms, and it is not unusual for one of them to take a good fish or two.

You would not believe the intensity that goes into the salmon fishing in Wales. The real salmon men are dyed-in-the-wool wormers and expert at it. They will be out at 3.00 a.m. or 4.00 a.m. in the summer to make sure they claim the best pool. (They've got to be up so early because the competition has to be seen to be believed.) Often the salmon are sold: with a lot of men here the fishing is something of a commercial enterprise, and many of them at least want to get back the price of their season ticket. In the old days, they would even take sack-loads of kelts away and sell them, but at least you don't see that sort of thing going on any more.

Another change that I should mention is that I put back virtually all the sea trout that I catch, and so now do many others too. It's not unusual to see the odd salmon go back, certainly if it has any colour in it, and it is a hen fish in the autumn. There has been quite a bit of education up here, and it is beginning to show.

LOW-WATER WORMING

I'm not in the least embarrassed to say that my first salmon was taken on a worm, and I admit the method remains – after thirty-odd years – my favourite of all, certainly on a small river when visibility is great.

When I was eleven, my parents sent me, alone with my rods, on a train, to a hotel by a Welsh river. This, as you can imagine, was my first taste of 24-hour freedom. Nobody before had ever bought me a drink in a bar and no adult had ever asked my advice seriously until then, when in a minor way I became known as the river expert.

In such a valley of mystery and of total happiness my passion for fishing grew, if that were at all possible. Never before had I fished all night or heard the otters whistle or been so aware of the dance of moonbeams on quick water. I had never seen water look silver – not blue or grey – and I had not watched the dawn break or been out in the fields and woods and felt the dew falling around me.

The river never left me that week. It wound around the village, past the hotel, under my bedroom so that I could hear it whilst I slept. The water had melted from snows at two thousand feet and ran ice-cold and clear, and bred

Dashing, well-oxygenated waters (right) are perfect for parr.

and beckoned me to him. He pointed down through the clear water and there I could see the ghostly figure of a great fish – a salmon. He produced a noose of brass wire, and he found a stick, a sucker from one of the nearby trees. Then I can remember him virtually immobile, lying above the salmon. The rest is naturally confused – a shout, a struggle, a hail of silver water, and this great glamorous fish was lying before me.

He offered the fish to me, and I knew that it would be wrong to accept. He got annoyed and asked me what on earth he was going to do with it. I was just too mesmerized by the size of the fish to do or say anything in particular. He then hid it under bracken, and the plan was for me to take it back to the village with me after dusk had fallen. It seems that he was a well-known poacher and would be regarded with suspicion, whereas I in my shorts and six-inch-high wellingtons would pass as an innocent. I fulfilled the bargain and left the fish on the fringes of the river as he instructed. I never saw it or him again.

If I managed to escape that temptation, then I did not shrug off the lure of worming, the usual method practised by all the local fishermen. Having seen a salmon, having confidence now they were in the river, I became determined to catch one. I began to talk to the worm fishers in the bar and to follow them round on the riverbank for the next few days, learning everything that I could. I soon found that my carp gear would be perfect for the job, and it was sent down by the next post. I was told that worms could be found in a village chicken-run and with a little bit of sweat I was set.

I caught three salmon over the next weeks and lost a lot more. What I learnt stood me in good stead in years to come when I was back in Wales, in the West Country, in Ireland or on occasional Scottish rivers.

Stealth

I suppose, top of the list, I would have to say that stealth is the major weapon of the low-

hardy clean fish. The trout seemed to hang as if in mid-air and the sun cast their distinct shadow on the gravel at the bottom. No taint hid their colour, their chalk-white mouths as they chewed, their vivid red gills that flared now and again and their buttercup bellies and the fawn skins that looked the texture of velvet spangled all over with droplet of ruby-red wine. I was intoxicated with trout, and I saw my first salmon leap at dusk from the tail of a weir. There was a glimpse only, but a tangible sensation which became a real thrill in the twilight. I knew, now, where future ambitions lay.

A village youth took me under his wing, and I remember vividly, to this day, one August afternoon walking along the river as the sun shone. He took particular interest in some overhanging alders and crept around their trunks for quite a few minutes before he exclaimed

water wormer. All my worming in this way is done in summer, when the water is warm and low, and when the fish are in the shallowest, best-oxygenated water. Here they lie, very spooky indeed, and you will soon see just how precise their eyesight is if you do not creep and crawl, shuffle and slide in circumstances like this. Of course, they seem to be just as aware of vibration, shadow or sound. You cannot leave anything to chance. Remember, once you have spooked a salmon in the shallow lie, it will never return. In deep water, a frightened fish might circle round once or twice but probably return to its original spot – not so under these conditions.

Time of Day

A low river has to be approached very slowly, and your progress has to be as watchful as possible. I like to see the fish themselves, and once a salmon is spotted it is very frequently catchable. I find that I fish a worm to a visible salmon with far greater intensity and concentration than I do to blank water – even if it is full of attractive looking features. There is something about seeing that yard of quivering silver that really focuses the mind. The other good thing, naturally, is that you can present the bait correctly if you see the fish.

I have generally found that the most successful worming takes place at dawn and dusk. Possibly this is because the light is less intense, and I and my rod are less obvious. I know that many low-water fish are taken in the day, and there are many occasions when I will go out in the brightest of conditions, but there is still a definite increased movement amongst the fish at the beginning and end of the day as far as I am concerned. It is hard to explain in our words, but the salmon knows: it is the type of agitation and awareness that you do not see in a fish during the full daylight hours.

Worms and Hooks

In my experience it pays to vary the size and number of the worms on the hook. My first approach, generally, will be to try two medium lobworms over a fish. If this does not work, then I will go to three or four larger worms that manage to excite a response quite frequently. A response does not always equal a take, but once the fish are alert and actually looking around, a return to the smaller bait often takes a fish at once.

I have always used and will always use a single hook. As a boy I did not see two-hook rigs used, so I grew up having no need of them and have never found the lack a problem. Also, in my opinion, using two hooks makes returning a fish more risky. I tend to use a long shank hook of size 4 or 6. Many of the carp hooks on the market now fulfil the job perfectly and possibly the best are those made by the Drennan Company.

Method

My usual aim is to fish the worm a few inches above the bottom and to bounce it as close as possible round in front of the fish's nose. I always try to do without shot because it is irritating how many times shot will catch in the bottom shingle or stones and impede the progress – generally at the most vital moment. However, sometimes the depth and the speed of the current make it essential to put either one or two swan shot six or twelve inches up from the hook. Hardly ever is more than that required. If you have not bought shot for some years, make sure that you go out and buy some new, so that you can be sure it is lead-free. The use of lead shot is now of course illegal, so do not be caught out.

I have learnt that salmon virtually always lie by the side of or above or in front of a stone, a boulder, a tree stump or an obstruction of some sort, certainly in smaller rivers like these. If you cannot actually see the fish itself, then looking for one of these objects certainly will give you many a clue and a starting place. I always expected that salmon would lie behind snags, sheltering from the full force of the cur-

Worm fishing on the River Wye. Notice I am casting upstream to let the bait trundle past the fallen branches where I had seen a good fish lying in cover.

rent, rather like barbel do, but they don't – except very rarely. I've also been surprised over and over again just how close into the bank salmon will lie. It doesn't matter how carefully you approach, you will still see that depressing bow-wave off across the shallows that tells of another lost fish.

In my view this is the real skill of low-water worming: finding the fish, or at least reading exactly where they will be. Then, of course, you've still got to present the bait correctly in the perfect position, so anybody that tells you that the method is easy and that worming is inferior probably hasn't tried it for himself. A background of coarse fishing is useful, and the man who can trot successfully for roach will know exactly how to use the current. This is absolutely vital.

A long rod is a great help and allows you to mend the line or to hold it away from snags so that you can guide the worm to where you want it. You must place the worm exactly because

there aren't many salmon who will belt around the pool after a worm like a trout sometimes does. In my experience, light line is also useful – not so light that you lose a fish – but not the twenty-pound stuff you often hear recommended. It isn't that the heavy line puts a fish off in my experience (though it might if the salmon has been in the river a long time), it is rather that lighter lines are much easier to mend, to control and direct. Thicker lines catch the current more easily and tend to drag the bait here and there where you don't want it to go. In my opinion, especially for summer grilse, eight-pound line is quite sufficient in most of these small rivers, and I would only step up to ten if I saw some bigger fish moving around.

Preparing to Strike
The greatest excitement in those early days was to watch the salmon attack the worm. I remember times that I really felt my heart stop. My blood pounded round my head and my rod

shook so much that it was a miracle I could muster the strength for a strike. Often the salmon would grab at the worms and nip them or perhaps shake them a couple of times and then let go. (These are the gyrations on the line that you often feel when you can't actually see what is going on.)

It might well be the third cast before they would actually take the worms properly into the mouth and you would feel a solid draw on the line that tells you to strike. I don't like to delay the strike because that can very easily mean a hook in the throat or the gills and a dead salmon whether you want that or not. For all these reasons, it is desperately important to be in tune and in touch with your worm. It is fine if you can see what is going on very clearly, but generally you can't, so it is essential to hold the line itself in your reel hand when fishing the worm. Your fingertips are surprisingly sensitive and you will soon learn to feel what is going on through the line. Developing your fingertips gives you a whole new set of eyes and the excitement of a tingling take is something you will never forget.

I hooked two salmon in one pool one day (and lost them both), and I still remember the satisfaction I felt in thinking the approach through, though it was mixed with that knife of despair that the fish were lost. One fish was in close to the bank just by the side of the rock. It was an easy cast and an easy fish to get at whilst the other was way out and would require a certain amount of wading. I took the easy fish first, led it out of harm's way . . . and lost it.

I sat on the bank for ten minutes, recomposed myself and worked out a strategy for the more difficult fish. I found I could just dib the bait correctly if I waded as far as I could and held the rod way out from my body over the current. The fish took at once, fought for ten or fifteen seconds and again was lost but the lesson was learned: I now approach every pool like a chess game or a real, strategic exercise. Hugh Falkus is a great man at this. Read the piece in *Freshwater Fishing*, the classic he wrote with Fred Buller. You will see a diagram

on page 223 that is really extraordinary. I've never actually met a pool like this but the lesson is inescapable and riveting.

I think Falkus is such a good wormer because he is a true hunter. He is a brilliant Spey caster and a giant with the fly, but underneath it all he is a *fisherman* rather than a purist, and he knows outwitting a wild creature by any means is a challenge of mammoth proportions. You could not have a neater profile of the low-water wormer.

WORMS ON THE WYE

Most of my own worming has been done on comparatively small rivers – a far cry from a salmon water the size of the Wye. However, worming on this large river and others is a very popular and exciting way of taking fish, and it needs to be explored. Our guide for this is Mike Taylor, the owner of that excellent old fishing hotel on the middle Wye, The Red Lion at Bredwardine. It is something of a fairy story really. As a lad Mike used to travel down to the Wye and his passion was fishing for salmon along that very beat owned by the hotel. Grown up, Mike was able to buy this place of his childhood dreams and now ensures that it fulfils every desire for every type of angler.

The Right Tackle

The tackle Mike uses is quite straightforward – a nine- to eleven-foot spinning rod (I would go for the eleven-foot end of the range as it would just give that little bit more control). This is teamed with either a fixed-spool reel or a multiplier (multipliers have traditionally been the reel for the salmon angler but do not worry too much: they are very difficult to cast with a light weight, and fixed-spool is much better for that particular job). Line strength rather depends upon the condition of the water, the time of the year and the size of the fish that are moving through. For example, in the spring, when there are still some very big fish about

The Barle, tributary of the Exe, in late September when the small Exmoor salmon begin to run.

A dark Highland fish held for a moment before release.

(Opposite) Salmon fishing is not just about fish: the beauty that remains in the memory – and the soul – forever is a large part of the attraction.

The headwater redds of a Highland river where the remarkable story of salmon begins.

It is quite amazing what can be done with a salmon fly rod. I have personally witnessed a 200lb beluga sturgeon tamed on one – an experience that always gives me confidence when any size springer comes to the fly!

A typical Highland scene: Scottish weather with a prime Scottish fly water in the background.

A lovely Tweed fish.

Pike being culled from a Scottish salmon system. Small pike obviously do damage, but anglers should return the 10lb-plus fish that help to keep down the numbers of destructive jacks.

(Opposite) Fresh water roars down the falls and the salmon begin to move.

Catching fish in the loch calls for specialized techniques, often trolling.

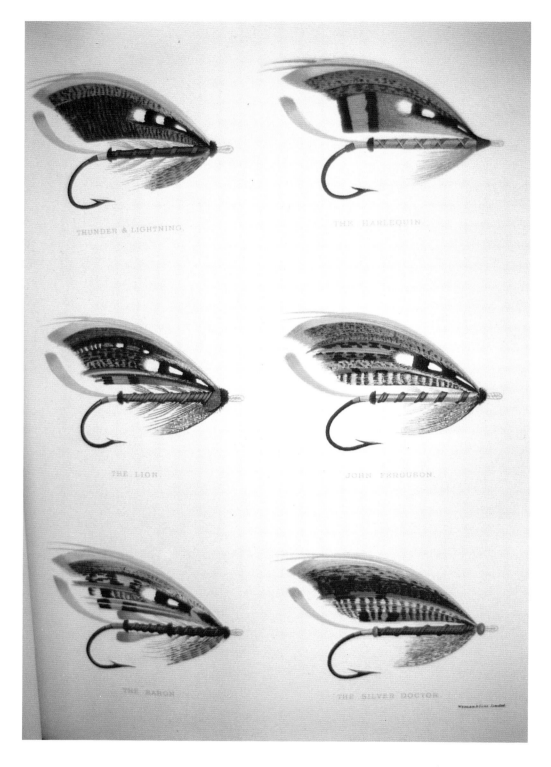

Pages of the past. Salmon flies of Kelson's day would certainly catch fish today.

THE BLACK RANGER

THE INFALLIBLE

BRITANNIA

JOCK SCOTT

THE CHAMPION

THE BLACK DOSE

Ernest Briggs' view of Loch Poulary; still a lovely salmon water, it has hardly altered over the last ninety years.

Poaching has long been a problem for salmon stocks.

The Edwardian salmon fisher: ladies have always excelled.

The last plunge.

Fine mahseer and salmon lies are almost identical.

A study of a 20lb mahseer, truly the Asiatic salmon, and one of the greatest challenges for the fly fisher.

Spring on the Tweed.

Happy – if wet – Norwegian days.

As part of a research programme, parr are kept in nets for scale readings and other tests. That fine fishery researcher Christopher West is in control.

A fine North American fish.

Salmon are stored in tanks before their eggs are stripped and they are released to make the long return to the sea.

Salmon are hoisted from the fish traps and prepared for stripping.

Glorious days on marvellous waters – the world of the salmon fisher.

(and I recently saw one that was way over thirty-five pounds), eighteen-pound line is generally used. In the summer, however, when the levels fall, the clarity increases and the fish tend to be smaller, you can obvious get away with a lower breaking strain. This does make sense because the thicker the line, the more difficult it is to manoeuvre the bait in an interesting fashion. The worms are mounted on a single barbed hook, generally either a size 4 or a size 6.

Mike uses a worming hook that has barbs on the shank. The key is to thread the worms up the hook, starting at the head. The barbs on the shank then keep them in place to stop them sliding down onto the bend where they look a lot more limp and drab. This really is quite important: it is vital to present the worm as enticingly as possible and a dull, limp affair won't take many fish. There's a certain amount of controversy whether a single worm is better than multiples of two, three or even four. Both methods are effective in their way, and no one can be sure about the mind of the salmon. However, as a rough guide, it makes sense to use two or three worms when the water is cloudy and perhaps a single worm in the heat and clarity of high summer.

Weight

We now come to the important issue of the weight. Why is it important? Well, it must be free-running in some way so that the salmon can take line without feeling the drag and rejecting the bait. A simple way is to have an eighteen-inch leader attached to the main line by a swivel. On the main line you simply place a running lead bullet. A better way is to fish the worm paternoster-style. Mike's gillies tend to use an eighteen-inch leader again beneath the swivel. Above the swivel a two-foot paternoster link is attached to the main line by means of a loop, a bead or a split ring. This means that the paternoster can slide up the line but not down towards the hook past the swivel. The weight is obviously put on the end of the paternoster link. The idea with this method is

One of the massive spring fish for which the River Wye was once so famous. This particular giant scaled well over 40lb.

that the worm will be fished between one and two feet off the river bed – that is out of the rocks and where the salmon are generally lying.

It is vital to get the weight part of the tackle right or you will miss many chances. The salmon, you see, will often pick up the worm and spit it out. It might circle round, come back, and go down and pick it up again. This can happen repeatedly. Once you feel the fish take the bait properly it is important not to strike at all. As Mike says, sit back, smoke a pipe or read a paper! The salmon is very likely to move around a fair distance once the worm is in its mouth. Then it takes it down more deeply. This can go on for at least a minute, and if you strike at the first indication, the fish will almost certainly be hooked in the lips and very probably lost.

You will generally know when to strike because the salmon will tell you! Once the worms are deep in the mouth, salmon tend to go a little bit wild as they feel the hook and often no strike is necessary. The line will move very forcefully at this stage, and you might well feel quite savage tugs. Sometimes the salmon will jump out of the water, and you will know that you are well and truly attached.

Where and When to Worm
Worming is a very skilful way of approaching Wye salmon, and you really have to make that worm search all the likely nooks and crannies. Avoid the big slack pools where worms would just sink to the bottom and be ignored. You need to investigate the edges of the main currents either along the side or towards the tail where the fish often lie. The worm needs to be active and bounce around, searching here and there for the salmon. This is active fishing, and you have to keep your mind totally on the job. In the summer when levels are low you will tend to find the salmon in the quicker, more lively water, whereas in the winter it might pay you to look in the deeper holes. Let the current do most of the work bouncing the worm around the river bed, but if you feel everything going dead and lifeless, then lift the rod tip and get the bait on the move once again.

Conditions are important, and the best time by far to fish the worm is when there is colour in the water. The Wye can rise very quickly – certainly over a foot an hour – but the good news is that it comes down just as fast. This is the crucial time when the level is dropping and the colour is beginning to go out. Clear water makes worming very difficult indeed, but when there is a nice tinge in the water you will find all the Red Lion men out.

Worms do not really work very early in the season although many anglers feel they should. According to Mike, the key is water temperature. In February or March the water is frequently so cold that it kills the worms within a couple of minutes, and without movement worm fishing is really useless. Thus, worming comes into its own from April onwards throughout the summer.

Specialized Equipment

When worm fishing, most salmon anglers simply adapt what salmon tackle they have, and this usually serves satisfactorily. However, if worming is a method that appeals to you greatly, it is probably worth buying more specialized tackle. For this you need to investigate the coarse fishing market where some beautiful rods are made. For example, Drennan International makes a thirteen-foot tench float rod which is absolutely superb for sensitive worm fishing for smaller salmon and grilse, certainly fish up to around ten pounds or so. The rod is light, delicate and precise and makes worm control a joy. For heavier fish, any of the modern carbon-fibre carp rods should prove quite excellent.

There are now many new-age fixed-spool reels that combine very well with their rods. The Shimano Baitrunner range is well worth looking at. It incorporates a facility that allows a taking salmon to remove line without any resistance. The reels are light, strong, reliable and a pleasure to use.

Obtaining Worms

It is the worms themselves that frequently cause the biggest problems and they can be bought in only a few places. Generally, it is a case of finding the worms for yourself. Possibly the most 'enjoyable' method of finding worms is by 'snitching' – the technique of going out on a warm damp night and picking the worms off the grass. You will see them stretched out with just a small portion of their tails in their holes. However, they are very sensitive, and even the lightest footfall causes them to disappear in an instant. It pays to have a bag or box ready and a good strong torch. Approach the worm carefully and grip it as close to the hole as you can. Then pull gently and steadily, and with luck it will come away unscarred. If the worm is bruised or bleeding, then discard it: if it goes in with its healthy colleagues, it will soon infect them all.

It probably makes sense to do as much snitching as possible before the fishing begins so that you have a good supply of worms ready. Storage need not be a problem, and the most useful thing for the job is a plastic tank – the sort that hold water in the average loft. Demolition sites are the places to get one or two for next to nothing. Once you have acquired the tank, drill twenty or so holes along the underneath and place four inches of fine gravel in the bottom. Put layers of newspaper over that, and then some soil, moss and even shredded newspaper. The gravel allows drainage and stops the worms leaving the tank altogether. After you have collected the worms, lay them on the top of the soil and leave them until the morning. Any worms that have not gone down into the tank should be removed as they will die eventually and kill the rest. Put the tank in a sheltered part of the garden where the sun will not hit it directly, and (in dry weather) water frequently. Also, turn the soil from time to time with a fork, and remove any suspect worms. If the weather becomes very warm, place a few turfs on top of the tank which will stop the soil drying out too quickly. Any worms left after your salmon trip should be returned and treated in just the same way as when they were caught initially. Once again, if any are unable to burrow down, discard them.

Creating a Wormery
An alternative is to create your own wormery in a shaded part of the garden. This need not be too large – around two yards square. Simply knock some stakes into the soil and fence the area in with planks. Dig the bottom out around twelve inches and lay a four- or five-inch layer of gravel to provide drainage. It is then just a job of filling this pen with manure, rotting compost and all manner of kitchen waste – especially orange peel, potato skins, lettuce leaves, pea shells and the like. Tea-leaves are supposed to be especially nutritious. Over the top, mole-hill soil can be placed and on top of that some turfs, again to keep in moisture. You will obviously have to stock the wormery

initially, but then the inhabitants will breed very quickly indeed. Lobworms are slower than brandlings, but after a year or so you will have a healthy stock growing, especially if you can feed it with all the kitchen titbits on a regular basis. A good wormery will provide all your bait needs for very many salmon seasons to come.

SALMON FISHING IN IRELAND

I devote quite a great deal of space to salmon fishing in Ireland for several, I believe excellent reasons. The first of these reasons is that salmon are very prolific in Ireland, certainly by comparison with Scotland. I can think of many salmon rivers indeed in Scotland where anything like a serious run is something out of the ordinary. This is not the case in Ireland, and it is possible, at some times of the year, to see so many salmon that it would gladden your heart and make you think that there is no shortage of them in the world whatsoever (though beware of these careless sentiments). The second reason is that by and large it is relatively cheap to salmon fish in Ireland. Some Irish salmon fishing is even free and excellent beats can be had for £10 or £15 a day. Despite this, Irish rivers are in no way crowded and very often you will fish for the day or the week alone. In both these ways, it is almost possible to return to the Scotland of the 1940s or 1950s in certain parts of Ireland. Thirdly, the Irish people are quite superb: forget all the stories of trouble and unrest and instead give yourself over to a nation that is full of kindness and cannot do too much to greet its visitors. Ireland is truly a land of beauty and plenty, and for the salmon fisherman it has virtually everything to offer.

The Advantages of Ireland

Richard Johnston lives in Dublin and works in the tackle industry. He is a crazily keen angler,

Ireland's top salmon waters: (1) Lough Conn and the Moy, Co. Mayo; (2) Lough Corrib and the Corrib, Co. Galway; (3) Lough Currane, Co. Kerry; (4) the Liffy, Dublin; (5) the Boyne and its tributaries, Co. Meath; (6) Lough Melvin and the Drowes, Co. Leitrim; (7) the Shannon, Co. Limerick.

and so by inclination and trade he is the person to tell everything about the Irish scene.

From the icy cold waters that surround the Irish coast, salmon converge on Irish river systems of all sizes, from the small spate rivers in the west to the larger rivers of the south. Just about everywhere in this enchanted Ireland, salmon are plentiful. Indeed, to us, these waters are a symbol of the quality of the environment in which we Irish are lucky enough to live. Still, it is salutary to remember that the Atlantic salmon depends on many factors for its survival. Most importantly, it needs a clean river to ascend and in which to spawn. Overfishing, both at sea and inland, is a threat to this most wonderful of fish.

Fortunately for us all, Irish waters are amongst the cleanest in Europe. Many of our rivers have never been tampered with by man in any way, so they are perfectly unspoilt for the salmon. Pollution cases, too, are becoming fewer and fewer, and this is due to heavy campaigning both by anglers and by the many wildlife groups. Agriculture used to be the main offender, but now the farmers' act has been tidied up considerably.

The net result of all this is that the visitor to Ireland has a huge choice of fishing, mostly on unspoilt waters where there are very few anglers indeed. It is not at all uncommon to fish for a week in Ireland and not see another angler. One can fish in the spring when the rivers are in full flow and try to outwit the big springer salmon, or one can choose to fish for the smaller, more numerous fish of the summer, known as grilse.

The Irish Waters

The Shannon

Irish salmon fishing goes back a long way, and at the turn of this century rivers such as the Shannon, Ireland's largest, were famous for their huge springers. One particular fishery on the Shannon at Castle Connell was the cream of them all. Anglers came from all over the world to fish here, and many were successful. Thirty-pound fish were commonplace and forty- and even fifty-pound salmon were taken

every season by anglers, both on the fly and the spinner. Unfortunately, a hydro-electric scheme was finally constructed over the Shannon, dramatically changing the environment for the salmon. Now, the forty- and the fifty-pound fish are just a memory, but it is still a very successful fishery, and plenty of smaller fish up to about twenty-five or thirty pounds are caught there every year. The Shannon also sees a vast run of grilse in the summer. The River Suir is another legend, and it was in this river that M. Maher caught the Irish record salmon in 1874 of a staggering fifty-seven pounds.

The Drowes

It is Ireland's grilse runs that are legendary, and rivers such as the Moy and the Drowes are unbelievably prolific. From May to the end of the season they can be teeming with salmon. Fantastic sport is had every year, and the beauty of the surrounding countryside brings anglers back, season upon season. In fact, to name all our salmon fisheries would take a whole book, but below is a breakdown of some of the best available to the visiting angler.

I will start with the Drowes in the northwest region of Ireland. This is a short river, only a little over four miles long, yet it provides anglers with sport from New Year's Day onwards. In fact, the first Irish salmon of the year is usually caught from the Drowes within minutes of opening. The river actually drains Lough Melvin and fishes best from March onwards. In 1989, for example, over 1,200 salmon were caught – just an indication of the fabulous sport that can be expected on such a short waterway.

Spinning and bait fishing are the best methods in the springtime, and lures such as the Flying 'C', Tobies of all sorts, Devons and Mepps are all favourites. In April, when the level drops, the grilse start coming in, and anglers begin to move to the fly. A double-handed salmon rod is useful on this river, but it is not a necessity and ten-and eleven-foot single-handed fly rods are used by most of the locals. The Drowes is not a very wide river, but waders are an advantage if you are going to cover all the lies available. Any selection of

Richard Johnston takes a few minutes out after a tiring day afloat on the Irish loughs for salmon.

salmon flies is a very personal thing, and who can say why a salmon takes a fly at all. However, I would recommend the various shrimp flies, a Hairy Mary, a Silver Rat, a Black Pennell or even a Garry Dog. All these flies should be tied very small for the summer fish in particular. Fishing is controlled by the owner of the river, Mr Thomas Gallagher at Kinlough, Coleitrim (Tel: 072 41208). The fishing is very cheap, and there is no limit to the amount of rods on the river each day, though it is never overcrowded in any way. The season runs from 1 January to the last day in September.

Lough Melvin
Lough Melvin is another great salmon fishery that is visited by a great many anglers each year. The fish enter the lake from the River Drowes itself. The water is famous for its many breeds of trout: it holds brown trout, gillaroo (the famous red fellow), sonighan trout and the mighty ferox. There are also many char and, of course, salmon. In the

spring, most of the fish are caught trolling with various spoons and spinners, the hot spot being Garrison Bay. In the summer months, salmon can be caught on the fly or even by dapping with normal trout gear, and this proves to be fantastic sport. The best flies seem to be Daddy-Longlegs, the Golden Bumble, the Bibio, the Black Pennell and the fly to have on the top dropper on every occasion is the famous Green Peter. Other noted areas on this lake for salmon are Laureen Bay and Rossinver Bay. Access for the visiting angler is excellent, and boats can be hired quite cheaply around the lake.

The Moy
The next fishery I would like to discuss is Ireland's (and probably Europe's) most productive salmon fishery: the River Moy. This river flows from the mountains of Mayo, through the lovely countryside, and out into the sea at the town of Ballina. This is where the famous Ridge Pool Fishery lies. Salmon

fishing in this pool is second to none, and if an angler hits the river exactly right – something that happens surprisingly regularly – he or she can catch literally dozens of fish in a single session. You might expect this pool to be very expensive to fish, but even at its peak it is only £50 for two rods a day, and an evening ticket can be purchased for around £12. What incredible fishing at such a reasonable cost! There is even a lot of free fishing upriver, and day-ticket water that hardly costs anything at all. Indeed, on average even the day tickets are quite frequently less than £10 a day.

Because of drainage work, much of the river is more suitable for worm fishing than spinning, although the stretches at Foxford and Swinford have some great fly water. In spring it is probably best to use worms or spinners for the salmon as the river can and often does run very high. Things do change, however, in the summer. A noted spot for holding fish is above the Ridge Pool where the fishery is only £5 a day – beat that if you can anywhere in Scotland. For information on the Moy, ring the fishery office in Ballina (Tel: 096 21332), and get up-to-date reports on the fishing. This office can also help with bookings. The season on the Moy runs from 1 February to 30 September.

Lough Conn

Upstream on the Moy is one of Ireland's greatest fisheries, Lough Conn. This lake is famous for its great trout and salmon fishing, especially in May and June when the lake sees a huge hatch of mayfly. Great numbers of salmon are taken here each year, and the action can be hectic in the early season as well as in the high summer. Locals troll baits in the spring and take the occasional fish, but when April comes, the number of fish really begins to increase. It is the summer fly fishing which brings the most salmon, and noted areas on the lake are Castlehill Bay and Mossbrook Bay. Artificial flies, such as Green Peter, Claret Bumble, Peter Ross and the Daddy-Longlegs will all take their fair share of fish. Dapping the natural daddy, grasshopper or even mayflies will take fish as well.

When there is a good wave on the lake, one should always dapp one or two flies across the waves, always diddling them, enticing the salmon up to take. Always remember to delay the strike with the salmon. This can be a problem on Conn and many of the Irish waters, as there are sometimes far more trout coming to the fly than salmon. However, if you want salmon, you should have a single-minded approach on a lake that holds both species. Boats and guest houses are plentiful around the lake, and local advice should always be taken.

Ballina is a great town for any angler in which to base himself: it has good access to fishing, fine pubs and restaurants, and very friendly people who will help in any way they can. As far as I'm concerned, the Moy system is definitely a salmon angler's paradise, and I am sure a single visit will lead you to agree with me.

Lough Corrib

In County Galway lies another fine salmon fishery. This is Lough Corrib, Ireland's second-largest lake. It is nearly thirty miles long and has a limestone base. Many rivers feed it, and many salmon come up from the sea at Galway Bay to spawn in them, running through the lough on their way. The first obstacle climbing salmon meet is the weir in Galway city – the famous Galway Weir Fishery. The level of the lake is controlled by the weir, and in the spring all of the gates are left open as Corrib spits out millions of gallons of water a day. In summertime, though, the majority of the gates are closed, and the pool below the weir can, at times, be full of salmon. Indeed, from the bridge a few hundred yards below the weir, many a passer-by can look out on hundreds of salmon below, all of them waiting to go upstream. The fishery here is controlled by the Western Regional Fisheries Board and is booked by letter. Again, like most fisheries in Ireland, it is very cheap to fish and a day in peak season for two anglers costs about £50. An evening session is very easy to book and costs a mere £8.

All methods are used, but spinning seems to take most of the spring fish. In summer, when the levels are low, you can wade into the pool and fly fish, and have some sport! If you

The grand old man of freshwater angling – E. C. Alston. This photograph was taken by Fred Buller during a last angling holiday, in Ireland of course.

should catch five or six fish a day, don't think you're doing anything fantastic! The fishery also has a regular gillie who will help you a great deal and point you in all the right directions. The overall atmosphere is very relaxed, and you would never believe that you were in one of Ireland's major cities.

When the salmon leap the weir and go upstream, they have only a few miles of slow water to travel before they reach Lough Corrib. Anglers troll this huge expanse of water and take salmon, quite a few of them very large fish, in the early season. Local knowledge is very important, and I would say that a gillie is a must. Because the lake is so vast, you have to realize that finding salmon is the first and major task. However, the locals

know every single fish-producing spot, and they will never give up trying to get you a fish. The way these guys work is amazing – often in terrible weather that makes you, the visitor, want to turn in as fast as possible.

The baits to use in the early season are the Yellow-Bellied Devon, the Flying 'C' – especially in reds and yellows – and any sort of Toby. The old favourite on Corrib was a silver-and-copper Toby Salmo, but tragically this is no longer available.

You will generally find that the holding areas for salmon in lakes like this are found off rocky points, off corners of islands and around the river mouths. In the early season, places such at the Narrows, Oughterhard Bay and Rabbit Island will all hold salmon in numbers. When trolling, you may even pick up a ferox trout, for they are present in large numbers in the lake. These are magnificent fish and can grow in excess of twenty pounds. In 1991, for instance, a $21\frac{1}{2}$-pound fish was taken in Outerhard Bay – a prize at least as great as the largest salmon.

When the mayfly appears, anglers flood there from all over Europe to sample some of the best mayfly trout fishing imaginable. However, salmon figure quite frequently in these catches and many of them fall to the dapp. Still, even in the summer, you will pick up fish on the troll in Oughterhard Bay and places like Greenfields.

Corrib is truly a mighty lake, so beware when the weather is rough. Take every single precaution as some of the rocks are the size of double-decker buses, and they can split a boat in two instantly if you should hit one. The season for salmon on Lough Corrib runs from 15 February to 30 September.

Lough Currane
It is the south of Ireland that has the country's most famous sea trout fisheries. Lough Currane is probably the star, but this also sees a great run of salmon. Currane is known worldwide, and it produces more specimen sea trout than any other Irish fishery. Sadly, in the last year or so, the runs of sea trout have collapsed, as have many in the other Connemara fisheries. There are many differing views on the cause of this tragedy, but the most likely one,

I believe, is the existence of the fish farms in the estuaries. These are breeding so many fish that the numbers of sea lice are exploding and beginning to attack the sea trout as they enter the estuaries and wait there to ascend rivers. Let us all hope that this terrible problem will be solved as soon as possible.

Thankfully, the salmon do not seem to be affected. Springtime offers a chance of a very large fish indeed to trolling, although even then anglers persist with the fly and do catch some fine fish. The baits to troll in this lough are the Toby, the Lukki Spoon, the Flying 'C', and lately some good fish have been caught on Tasmanian Devil Lures – mostly blue and silver.

Lough Currane is a free fishery, and launching your own boat is no problem at all. If you are fishing there for the first time, however, it really would make sense to use a gillie. The town of Waterville is full of fishermen who would gladly take you out for a reasonable fee. In the warmer months, the grilse arrive and can be taken on the fly or (as many people love to do) on the dapp once again. The dapp accounts for many salmon, and there is always a chance of a large sea trout falling to the method. You can fish Currane from 17 January until 30 September, and fish will be there through the season. In 1986, over 350 salmon were caught on fly alone.

There is a short river running from Lough Currane to the sea, which is controlled by the Butler Arms Hotel. The beats are private, but if you are staying at the hotel, you can fish them right down to the sea. The countryside around Waterville is unbelievably splendid, and the mountains and lakes combine to present one of Ireland's finest landscapes.

The Boyne
In the east of Ireland lies one of our premier waterways, the Boyne system. This river is over seventy miles long, covers three counties and flows into the sea at Drogheda. Spring fishing is the big attraction on this river, and a noted spot is Navan, where the Blackwater meets the Boyne. This area is called the Mollies and has produced many thirty-pound salmon over even recent years. Yellow Bellies, Tobies and most other lures all work well on

the river. There are many private fisheries and syndicates on the river, but a lot of day-ticket water is available as well.

In summer, there is a good run of grilse to ten pounds or so, and both spinning and fly fishing will be well worthwhile. The Boyne is a large river, so a double-handed fly rod will probably be useful sometimes with a sinking line. The flies to use are Thunder and Lightning, the Garry Dog and various other local favourites which you will find out about by asking almost anybody! This river nestles in some of the richest land in Ireland and is a magnificently picturesque place to fish. Its tributary, the Blackwater, sees a few fish as well each year and is well worth trying in the early season especially.

The Liffey
When talking about Ireland, I must mention the River Liffey. It is not a prolific water by any standards, but it does deserve a few words. Rising in the Wicklow Mountains, it flows through County Kildare and on into Dublin city, where it meets the sea. Being in the capital city, it was used for industry, particularly for shipbuilding, and never really had a chance to make its name as a salmon fishery. None the less, hard work by the fishery boards and the angling clubs paid off, and it is now becoming a cleaner, nicer river and starting to be recognized again. It has often boasted the first salmon of the season in Ireland, and there are plenty of accessible beats – one of the most prolific of them being a stone's-throw away from the city centre itself. This is Ireland Bridge, and one can actually fish there for a mere £30 a season!

The local club, the Dublin and District Salmon Anglers, looks after the stretch very well.

DAPPING FOR SALMON

I met Des Elliott in the most bizarre of circumstances. Fred Buller had been generous enough to lend me his cottage on the banks of Lough Mask for a stormy week at the beginning of the season in 1990. What I did not know was that Des Elliott, the Dublin architect, also had a key to the cottage, and for the first two or three days of my stay I was perturbed to find that the fire would sometimes be lit when I came back from fishing or that something had been moved or taken. However, there was no sign of anybody else in the house. If this were a haunting, I began to feel it was a very friendly one indeed. Eventually, to my relief, Des revealed himself, and I instantly recognized a very fine and passionate fisherman.

My own particular purpose in going to Ireland at that time was to fish for the great ferox trout in the lough, and Des is a famed captor of these (in fact the very first morning I saw him, he also happened to have a ten-pounder under his arm!). However, it was to the dapp that Des was particularly keen to introduce me, and so it came about on a Wednesday afternoon, in a screaming westerly gale, that Des, Joy and I set out to dapp on a bay of Lough Mask.

It was a crazy thing to do, and the waves were crashing in over four or five feet high, I swear. I have never before felt seasick on a fresh water in a small boat, but I did that day, and the eight-inch trout we finally managed to outwit did nothing to take my mind off my woes. Joy stuck it out, and I take my bobbly hat off to her!

I recount this experience to show that nothing deters Des, and if anybody knows the western loughs, he does. Here are his comments on dapping for salmon.

A Local's Guide

You must understand that the Corrib dappers are out there first and foremost for trout during the mayfly season. Salmon do come along, but they are not as frequent as trout, and really they are seen as a bonus. Sea trout and brown trout come by the score, but if you are going to catch salmon there really has to be a prolific run on at the time. When that happens, you do see a good number of salmon come back that have fallen to the method. In fact, I can remember times when one fish in six has been a salmon – fresh-run at that. They are generally grilse. There's no particular reason why, other than that grilse runs and mayfly hatches tend to coincide. I am quite sure bigger, spring salmon would take the mayfly on the dapp well, but it is grilse that happen to be running most prolifically at that particular time.

Tackle

Because we are generally after trout or perhaps sea trout at the time, tackle might sound a bit on the light side, but most fish that are hooked are landed. A size 10 hook is the thing, but it must have a wide bend to take the two natural mayflies you put on it. Simply hook them through the thorax, and they should stay on. Mayflies are so prolific, that you can pick them off the bushes around the lake shore before you start fishing. It's as easy as that providing they are out in numbers. If they are not, you could have problems and that's why there is a thriving schoolboy industry on Corrib! The kids collect them and then sell them to the anglers the next day. I'm not sure what the going rate is at the moment, but I guess it's somewhere between 50p and £1 for a dozen – you probably have to bargain a bit with them. Make sure the flies are in decent condition.

Telescopic fibreglass rods seem to be all the rage, generally extending to about fourteen feet in length. The good thing about the rods being telescopic is that if the wind becomes very strong and the full rod is difficult to manage, then you can ship down a section and fish with a rod of reduced length. This is a system that works very well indeed.

I recently fished with Hugh Miles, the celebrated film maker and noticed that for one of his roaching techniques, Hugh used an enormous telescopic rod of around eighteen or twenty feet in length. This was very light, even at this length, and it struck me at the time as an excellent potential dapping tool. I am also surprised that neither Des nor Richard in his article on Ireland commented on the new carbon-fibre rods now available. For example,

I have a fourteen-foot carbon-fibre tench rod made by Peter Drennan that hardly weighs anything at all, is thin as a wand and tremendously responsive. Surely such a tool would catch the wind very little and be manageable in most conditions. It is so light that you can hold it all day and feel no fatigue at all.

Centrepin reels are used uniformly with plenty of nylon backing of about fifteen-pound breaking strain. To this is attached a length of synthetic floss anything between ten and twelve feet in length. To that is attached the leader which will be something between four and eight feet of nylon of about six-pound breaking strain. These are rough measurements because they tend to be changed according to the weather conditions. For example, in a very stiff wind you probably won't need the floss which is only there to help catch the breeze if there isn't much of it about. Equally, you can use a slightly heavier leader because hardly any, if any, is put on the water.

Technique

The trick is to let the flies sit on the water and drift ahead of you, in front of the boat. You can lift them off from time to time and let them settle again totally naturally, but that is the key. Your natural mayfly has to behave as much like the real thing as you can make it.

A drift on a water the size of Corrib can cover miles, and you will be passing over many scores of fish as you go. However, this can be a frustrating way of fishing. For example, supposing you see a good fish – salmon or trout – move right or left of your drift. If you are on your own, then there's very little that you can do except let your fly move directly in front of you. Ideally, you need two men dapping and one man on the oars, so that he can redirect the boat if you see a really good fish that you want to go after.

The fish move upwind, and you will see them rising, taking the naturals in a lazy way. Yours is very likely to be accepted providing it does not skitter along the surface or look unnatural in any way. At this time of the year there is no doubt that the dapped mayfly beats a wet fly hands down and brings in whole baskets of fish, grilse included. Moreover, it's a fascinating and satisfying way to fish. After all, you are imitating nature to the utmost degree.

NORWEGIAN SALMON

In 1991 a friend phoned to tell me of some salmon fishing he had just experienced in Norway. He made me promise that I would never reveal in print the basic facts of what he was going to tell me, so special was the journey he had just enjoyed. However, he had no complaints about me telling the story if the river and other giveaways were kept secret. The tale really is so beautiful that it must be told in order to give a true reflection of what Norwegian salmon fishing was once like and can still be today. Apparently my friend and his party (seven others) had to travel the last two hours of their long journey by horse and cart because there was no tarmacked road into this upper valley. They found themselves following the river ever higher, where it opened out into a wide, seemingly endless floodplain between steep hillsides. Here and there were dotted white cottages, summer residences for Norwegians who came up to tend cattle or simply escape the city. The whole valley was a profusion of wild flowers, and the sun beat down on a crystal-clear, dancing blue river.

The party was shown to a delightful house, spotlessly clean, with all manner of exotic foods on a trestle table, under covers to keep away the flies. There was a ready supply of wine in a cooling bin nearby, and the bedrooms looked out over the river. The next week was quite obviously the paradise time of my friend's life. His friends and he came and went, fished and slept, ate and drank, and talked and laughed just as they wished. During every hour of the twenty-four some would be fishing and some would be sleeping. It was a constant, shifting pattern, with people waking, walking to the river, catching salmon and returning. It was the sort of freedom most of us can only remem-

Just an indication of what Norwegian salmon can be like.

ber from childhood and that alone would have made the week special.

The fishing made it utterly unforgettable. Apparently, everybody fly fished. The river cried out for it, being broad, shallow, quick and clear. The salmon were forging in, fresh and bright, and taking flies with abandon. In that quick water, these silver fish fought like demons, and when you hear that their *average* size was twenty-six pounds, you will guess why my friend insists I keep this location private. Out of the eight fishermen, all but one landed fish over forty pounds, and they all had numerous thirty-pounders. (Remember that all came to the fly.) My friend said that it really was with tears in his eyes that he left the river at the end of that week and at once began to make plans for his return. That is why he phoned me. He wanted to know if I would care to be a member

of his party? Would I care! I would have died for it; if I could have found the £7,000 necessary for the experience – £1,000 a day! You would not dare have a hangover and miss a morning at that price! I am still saving up, confident that one day I will see that flower-spangled valley and those white Norwegian houses high on their hillside.

The Early Days

It was the English to a great degree that helped pioneer salmon fishing in Norway on those rivers whose names still ripple with pure magic – the Vosso, the Alta, the Namsen and the Laerdal. Indeed, it was in the 1830s that Reverend Bilton made his first two journeys to the Namsen with shattering results. Soon *Jones' Guide to Norway* began to give practical advice and describe the sort of journey these early anglers could expect to make.

The steamer from London to Hamburg alone took sixty hours and from there the angler travelled by land to Kiel. Then a steamboat would take him to Copenhagen and then on to Oslo. After Oslo the steamboat would move on to Trondheim, calling in at every little bay and waterside frontage – often over sixty of them! From Trondheim a carriage would take the angler – at walking pace – across very wild country. Apparently, the whole journey could take almost a month, and that was if the angler had the strength of mind to avoid the wild night life of Hamburg!

Even when the rivers were reached, this was not the end of it, for there were no facilities laid on for these earliest anglers. It was very much a question of living rough and taking all food and camping equipment along. Reindeer skins and axes were essential equipment, along with the inevitable brandy flask and a mixture of hogs' lard and spirit of turpentine to keep away the desperate midges.

These early fishermen certainly suffered for their sport, to the extent of using nineteen-foot rods made with hickory, ash, lance wood or laminated split bamboo. For the really big rivers twenty-four-foot rods were recommended, creations that measured five inches around the butt and weighed in at a total of five pounds! After a month's travelling, and weeks of camping, imagine using one of those day-long on a fast spate river!

Still, the rewards were quite stunning, certainly enough to attract members of the British aristocracy again and again, year after year. Amongst the most successful of the British anglers was Viscount Coke, whose sporting records still reside at the family home of Holkham Hall in Norfolk. These make fascinating reading.

Salmon fishing history.

The Situation Today

Obviously, from my opening story, Norway still has rivers with excellent beats that can offer the best Atlantic salmon fishing in the world. However, the great days on all Norwegian salmon rivers are to a great extent in the past, and the traveller of today has to be selective if he is going to fulfil the journey of his dreams. The decline set in around the later 1970s, and the Norwegian government took drastic action. Norwegian drift-nets were suspended and poaching was vigorously discouraged for the first time in Norwegian salmon history.

However, problems still remain because most of the rivers in Norway are owned by farmers, and many of them understand little of the art or importance of sport fishing. They see the river merely as a resource to be used and milked and put precious little back in terms of care or maintenance. Of course, this is a generalization tragically applicable to many rivers. Catch and release is pretty well unknown to most of these riparian owners, and subtlety of method is equally ignored. Rod numbers can be high, and on many rivers use of the worm, prawn and spinner is commonplace. Fishing on both banks is also the norm.

Securing a Good Beat

There are some bright spots, however. Many associations, companies and individuals have bought up stretches on long leases and are making great headway in reconstituting pools and spawning redds. In short, Norwegian fishing is very much a matter of chance: you can find yourself on an excellent beat or a useless one. The deciding factor, very often, is money.

Money and Norwegian salmon fishing go hand in hand, and finance is one of the most delicate of subjects. The world recession that looks like drifting on into the next century has obviously had an effect on the rents that owners can expect to receive for their salmon fishing, and prices have been kept in some sort of check. However, there are several dubious operators in the field who have tended to charge very high rents for mediocre beats, hoping that the measures taken by the government will pay off quickly. This has not been the case: salmon fishing that has been run down over many years takes time to resuscitate, and many people have paid sky-high prices only to find rivers with very few salmon running.

The really important message here is to make sure that whatever you pay, the river you choose has had good references. It is essential to check on catch rates over the previous years and not take for granted any glib promises by commercial operators. Many of the best fishing beats are secured by personal contacts, and the largest cheque book in the world cannot guarantee entrance to this type of fishing.

By and large there are several additional ways to secure salmon fishing in Norway, and the first is to buy day-ticket fishing. This can be very reasonably priced and often of excellent quality, and the real bonus is that you are not committed to a certain stretch for all your stay. If the fishing isn't spectacular, or good even, then it is very easy to be up and off to pastures new. Approaching Norway in this way, especially for the first time, also lets you see the country, sample several different river systems and be in a better position to make decisions in future years.

Another way is to buy a rod on an acknowledged beat at what is considered a good time of the year. This is the safe way of approaching things, but it is, of course, an expensive route. You would expect to pay anything approaching £3,000 for this privilege – a sum beyond the pockets of many. At least you will be pretty sure of getting value for money, and it is probably a good idea to do this – if you have the money – in the first place, so that you don't fall into the hands of one of the commercial operators that charge a high rate for mediocre fishing. In short, it is better to go for either the cheap end of the market or to the very top if your pocket extends this far. Of course, if you have heard good reports of an operator, it might pay you to follow up on what he has to offer.

When to Fish

Whatever route you choose, remember that by and large the best seasons in Norwegian rivers depend upon their altitude and how the rivers are fed. As a generalization, the top season tends to run through June and into mid- or late July. Most people would agree that these are the weeks to aim for if you have a choice. Norway is, of course, renowned as the 'Land of the Midnight Sun', and many fishermen have had their greatest successes at night. Indeed, on some rivers, fishing only begins after dinner and continues right through until dawn or beyond. This is romantic stuff, but it is not always the case. On some rivers, the daytime sun melts the snows in the mountains and through the night the river rises and cools down, and sport is patchy. In short, you have to know your river and follow local advice and customs.

Tackle

It pays to remember that Norwegian fish can run very large, and you do not want to run any risks with your tackle. Most people agree that twenty- or twenty-five pound nylon should be the minimum leader strength, and that the rod should have sufficient backbone to cope with very big fish in quick currents. The reel, too, should be large enough to hold at the very least a hundred yards of backing, for often the fish will set off on a seemingly unstoppable run. Most fishing is done with sinking or at least semi-sinking lines, and flies tend to be big throughout the season. However, fast-sinking, heavy tube flies are not generally considered best for Norway, and most travellers prefer a fly that retains some life in the water and looks that little bit more natural.

SALMON IN LABRADOR

I feel as if I know the Labrador Atlantic salmon scene almost as well as I know the Scottish one,

Jim Deterding with a superb Norwegian salmon taken on the spoon.

simply because so many of my friends have gone there and returned with all manner of stories, photography and video tapes. I suppose my great friend Shirley Deterding is the most frequent visitor, and she always describes her trips in the most enthusiastic of ways. Basically, she loves wilderness fishing, and she glories in Labrador because of the Atlantic Salmon, a fish she has grown up with and with which she identifies. Her favourite place is Michael's River, which is about a 1½-hour flight in a float plane from Goose Bay. All in all, it takes Shirley around two full days of travel to reach Goose Bay from the east of England. However, she had to rely on the weather, and fog can close in almost instantly and block off her entry or exit. I think it is the approach into Goose Bay that stuns her as much as anything – those seemingly endless miles of tundra, acres of wild beauty that has probably hardly ever seen a human foot of any size or description. It is a truly wild place, and in the winter the snow drifts to the chimney pots of the cabins, the temperatures sink to minus forty and plastic beakers shatter if they are dropped.

The beauty of the place attracts Shirley because, after all, she is a renowned artist. She loves the colours of the white sand, the blue ocean and river and the opaque glint of the icebergs around the bay, with the accompanying whales and seals. She likes to paint the endless variety of wild duck, snow geese, eiders, loons and the host of shoreline birds that dazzle in the bright air. From what she says, I sometimes think she has difficulty in deciding whether to take up the rod or the palette.

Even when fishing, the wildlife experience continues with osprey, bear, moose, caribou, fish-eagle and long-eared owls. This is a land of animals and tranquillity. The fishing obviously is extraordinary, and there is nothing Shirley likes better than motoring in a small boat upriver from the camp by the bay, fishing the pools as she goes, secure in the knowledge that hardly ever is a line cast upon them. It is common to take lunch by the river side, and a small grilse will be skilfully cooked by an Indian guide. Apparently, many lunches last too long simply because of the grey jays, the Whisky Jacks, that hop round the fire eager for bits of fish skin or morsels of bread. They delight Shirley with their display of confidence and cheekiness.

According to Shirley Labrador Atlantic salmon take and fight with far more spirit than almost any other salmon you are likely to find in Scotland. Shirley is a great believer in the use of a light trout rod with small single-hook flies, rather than heavier, more traditional Spey-type tackle. After all, most of the fish are grilse. Every now and again, a proper salmon will be hooked, and taking a sixteen-pounder in freezing water on light tackle is an experience that you will never forget.

However, not every Labrador experience is a good one, and there have been times when Jim (her husband) and Shirley have come back very frustrated with the entire trip. If you time things too soon, or the warm weather comes late, then you can find the bay frozen, and the fish keeping out of the river. You know there are tens of thousands of fish waiting to go up, but it is of no use. You have spent the money, and all you can do is sit back and wait.

The Labrador Season

Fishing starts when the ice melts from the rivers, generally around mid- to late June. Probably the first fish to run once the rivers are free of their ice are char, moving in with the larger salmon. All this takes place in May or early June, and this is probably the prime time because by August the smaller male salmon and the grilse are really beginning to flood in. Those first two or three weeks after the ice has gone represent the real hot period, but things can change according to latitude, and the temperatures in Labrador can vary immensely. If you are thinking of going, it is absolutely imperative to obtain the vary best advice that you can pay for.

Most of the fishing on the rivers of Labrador takes place around the estuaries, but the season can be extended by moving upriver to lodges in the true wilderness, where salmon will be encountered again close to the spawning beds, having lost some of their silver and most of their sea lice. If it is a really active fresh fish that you want, stick close to the sea. By September things are slowing down very quickly before the onset of the next, terrible winter, but like on Scottish rivers, this is a good time to catch the occasional very big fish if you have the nerve to try it.

Equipment

Most of the Labrador rivers are very wide, quite shallow and quick flowing, not dissimilar to the Dee or stretches of the Tay, and the sort of

Tide bright fish come in from a freezing sea.

gear that you would use there is quite adequate. However, as I said earlier, there is a strong move to fish the American way with much lighter gear. Another East Anglian friend of mine, Richard Gibbs, also stresses this choice. Richard organizes many trips each year out to Labrador, and he says that the clients who get most from the experience are those who fish light, keep on the move and are in constant contact with their fly and the river. Richard describes it as an 'on-the-toes' approach, and he despairs when he sees fishermen settle into an unthinking, unfeeling rhythm.

Watching videos of Richard is quite an experience. He is nothing like a human heron – far more of a dipper! He flits from here to there, popping a fly behind a rock into a small pool into a quick run, and then he is off again. The thinking is that these are very active fish,

very much on the move, and flogging a pool is not of great use. The fish will either be there or not, and if they are there, they are likely to take almost at once. Thus, if you are without success after the first few casts, move on and on until the fish are found.

Richard always seems to wear chest waders because these allow him to get to the very best places that many would leave alone. It's interesting to note that he generally has with him a spare pullover or two because, apparently, the saying goes in Labrador that 'If you don't like the weather, wait half an hour and it will change'. For the same reason, if you can get a thin waterproof in your bag, it is not a bad idea.

Wildlife

When you are in a wilderness area, there are one or two things that you should consider. Remember that bears are very common, so it would be stupid to leave a fish on a rock where one will almost invariably take it if your back is turned for long. (If the bear does not appear, then an otter or a seal will.) If a bear comes your way, leave him to it – do not argue with a fellow like that. Nor should you argue with the midges. They can be very vicious unless you are actually in mid-river or near the coast, where the breeze often leads them away. If you go into the interior on a muggy day, you are asking for trouble.

The Cost Factor

Trips to Labrador are not cheap. They worked out at over £2,000 a head in 1993. Generally, the price is going to be more than this, and you have all the extras to take into account as well. If two of you are going, expect little change out of £5,000. This amount of money would buy you quite a few weeks in Scotland, even at one of your favourite hotels in prime season. The question is whether you will actually catch any fish while you are in Scotland, and certainly more than half a dozen for the week would be quite something. You can better this tally in a couple of hours in Labrador in quite exhilarating surroundings.

All sorts of questions come into play. Will,

Scenes like this are still common today in Labrador.

for example, the wilderness experience and the sport offered by these exceptional fish spoil you for ever more? Will you no longer be satisfied with the comparatively tame fishing of Scotland once you have tasted a fresh Labrador twelve-pounder. I don't think this is the case at all. Most anglers are able to separate the two experiences and value each for what it offers. Certainly, Labrador is an experience every salmon angler should try at least once in his life. I can't wait for my first visit, hopefully coming soon!

DISCOVERY OF THE KOLA

I suppose without any shadow of a doubt the most exciting development to take place in salmon fishing in the last ten years is the discovery of the unexploited salmon stocks in the Kola peninsula. All reports over the last four or five years seem to indicate that here is salmon fishing of the sort that our grandfathers knew and would recognize. For those of us who have struggled for weeks of our salmon fishing lives for the odd fish, a take even, or just the sight of a leaping salmon, then the Kola must offer rewards beyond all our dreams.

The Swedes have pioneered the Kola more than any other country, and a company called Flyfish in Kola has taken charge of both the fishing and the camps on both the Strelna and Chavanga rivers in the south-east of the peninsula. All accounts seem to suggest that this area has the most productive salmon fisheries in the world today, and the camps are open from late May until the middle of October. The area is certainly one of the most unspoiled and undeveloped areas in the world, and there has never been any industrial development whatsoever, so there is no pollution – the curse of so many other rivers in what was Russia.

The few people who do live in the area make their living solely from hunting, fishing and farming. The Kola peninsula is roughly the size of Scotland – about 250 miles long and 115 miles wide. There are 110,000 lakes and 20,000 rivers on the whole peninsula, and fishermen from all over the world have travelled there since the late eighties and been utterly staggered by what they have found. The camps own cows. Add to all this any fish caught during the day, and local sea fish as well, and you can see that you are not going to starve in any way. The camps also offer small but clean log cabins with hot washing facilities, showers, saunas, toilets and generated electricity for smoke houses and freezers. (One or two of the camps even offer satellite television – something that I am not sure the remoteness of this area really calls for.)

The camps tend to be sited on some of the best fishing areas, and there are frequently good pools within walking distance. Nevertheless, most camps have a daily helicopter service which provides fast and easy transportation to all the rivers in the area. Also, the camps have good boats with outboard motors that are available for short trips along the coastline. Rubber rafts for drift fishing the rivers are also available. For most people, each week will include one or two days with the helicopter, flying to the upper reaches of particular rivers, and then the anglers will float downstream, fishing where they like. This is an excellent way of fishing water that is totally virgin as well as seeing the outstanding natural beauty of the region.

The climate and the mosquitoes have frequently drawn much comment from visitors. The mosquitoes generally arrive in late June and are around in variable quantities until late August. They can be hellish, but during cold windy weather they will generally disappear. If the angler goes well prepared and has a good repellent, there should not be too many disastrous problems. The Arctic summer offers the midnight sun, and temperatures vary from around ten degrees centigrade to twenty-five degrees centigrade. Rainfall is normally light in the summer, but at less latitude the weather can change very quickly indeed, so it is well to take some waterproof clothing.

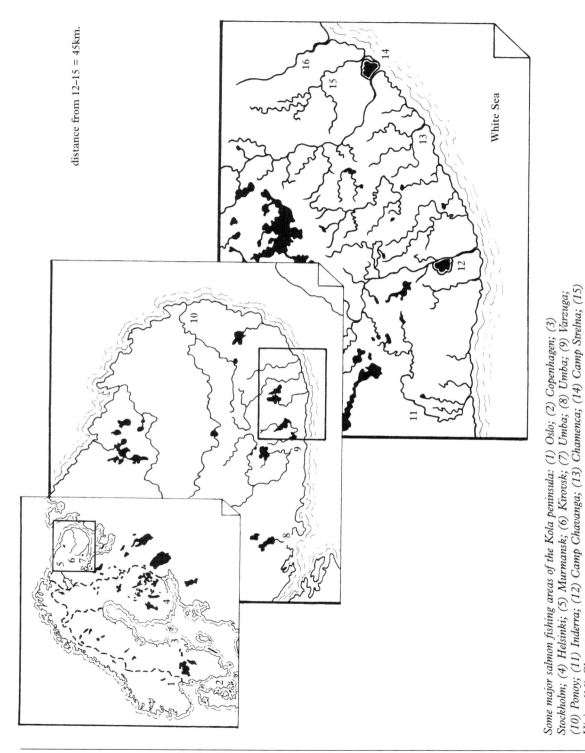

distance from 12–15 = 45km.

White Sea

Some major salmon fishing areas of the Kola peninsula: (1) Oslo; (2) Copenhagen; (3) Stockholm; (4) Helsinki; (5) Murmansk; (6) Kirovsk; (7) Umba; (8) Umba; (9) Varzuga; (10) Ponoy; (11) Inderra; (12) Camp Chavanga; (13) Chamenca; (14) Camp Strelna; (15) Uigin; (16) Chapoma.

The Kola Rivers

The best-known rivers are the Umba, the Strelna, the Chavanga, the Chapoma and the Inderra, with two of the best of the smaller rivers being the Kamenka and the Uigin. Most of these rivers are around twenty to fifty yards wide and offer perfect fly fishing conditions: the water is generally shallow, rapid and very clear, and the sea is never far away, so constant runs of fresh fish are almost assured. Almost every camp in the Kola has virtually unfished rivers nearby, so there is always that thrill of the unknown – a real opportunity for the adventurous to discover new pools and maybe even whole rivers.

The character of the rivers will remind many anglers of the rivers of Ireland or northern Norway. They all originate in the Tundra Plateau which is well above sea level, and this gives an excellent rate of flow with miles of perfect fly water, boasting fast rapids and long pools. The water comes from an endless area of peat bog, which gives the water just a tinge of brown. One of the secrets of the good fishing on the Kola is that the peat bog acts as a giant sponge, releasing the waters slowly throughout the whole season. As a result, the water level in the rivers falls and rises fairly steadily. The vegetation around varies from oak and tundra, to forest with pine, spruce and birch.

Kola Salmon

Kola salmon do not average a huge size, and the general run will be around four to sixteen pounds, with eight- and nine-pounders predominating, but of course this depends on the river and the time of the season that you are fishing. Each year, salmon of thirty pounds are caught, and there are excellent sea trout which can easily move into double figures. Most fisheries in the Kola are run on a catch and release basis, though anglers are allowed to kill two fish during their stay: one for the table and one to take back as a trophy or a celebration supper. For this reason, virtually all camps say that either single or double hooks are allowed, but they must be barbless. When the salmon are really running, some camps insist on the use of single hooks only.

I suppose it is the number of salmon here that blows one's entire mind in these days of salmon droughts. It is not unusual to hear of men catching ten salmon in a day, and that is all on fly. In fact, statistics seem to prove that the average daily catch on most Kola rivers is 4.3 salmon per person, but like everywhere there are those who struggle on certain rivers at certain times.

One of the great things about fishing the Kola is that it is generally possible to choose a river or beat that will suit you and your style of fishing. Some will provide easy walking and fishing alongside grass-banked pools, and others call for deeper wading with harder fishing perhaps in some deep gorges or canyons for the adventurous angler. Chest waders are essential and all the traditional methods work well. Kola salmon differ in only one respect: they are very prone to coming to the surface, and dry fly fishing can be excellent.

Equipment

It is probably wise to take a long traditional salmon rod, but for many of the smaller rivers a ten-foot trout rod will be quite adequate. However, most Kola regulars stress that a hundred yards of backing is absolutely essential. It seems that these Kola fish fight far harder than those of Scotland or Ireland, probably because of the strength of the water and its low temperatures.

Remember that a visa is obligatory for travel in the Kola (most tour companies will arrange that for you). Generally, language is not a problem, and all camps have guides that can speak a smattering of English. There will probably be a camp organizer who is fluent.

4 TAIL PIECES

SALMON FISHING'S HEROES

A local land owner I know has a library that holds just about every volume ever written on salmon fishing. It is immense, filling the wall of a huge room. It's easy to see why, because salmon fishing has always attracted sportsmen. The species represents an ultimate glamour. Big, fresh-run, hard-fighting salmon caught in wonderful surroundings are hard to resist. The list of successful salmon anglers over the past two centuries is equally overwhelming, to judge by their books: Kelson, Scrope, Hughes Parry, Balfour-Kinnear, Waddington, Ashley Cooper, Hugh Falkus, Neil Graesser, Crawford Little and many more from each generation. Arthur Oglesby, though, has probably been the most accessible of the genuine greats. He has a history of successes stretching back over twenty-five years or more.

An expert caster with a deep understanding of fish since the minnow traps of boyhood and an obvious love for what he does, Arthur could hardly have been expected not to take his opportunities both here and abroad. His books have acted as bibles for most newcomers to the salmon scene for over a decade, and I respect my copies for their intelligence and clarity. It should also be said that Arthur has made one positive, personal contribution to game fishing: with Roy Shaw – also of Yorkshire – he ranks as angling's best photographer, certainly in the game world. His photographs have graced books and journals for almost thirty years, and he has found what is a perfect balance between instruction and inspiration.

There are, however, two salmon anglers of earlier times of a type unusual in their brand

of angling: A. H. E. Wood and Robert Pashley. They are men who concentrated their fishing on one river, even one beat of the river, until they came to know the water with complete intimacy. It was only then that true progressions were made that changed the face of salmon fishing for many.

A.H.E. Wood

Seventy years ago A. H. E. Wood of Glassel, as J. W. Hills said, turned the salmon world 'topsy turvy'. Wood fished almost exclusively on the prolific Cairnton beat of the Aberdeenshire Dee and reintroduced there the concept of the greased floating line. Earlier experts like Laming and Grant had moved away from the constant use of a sunken line before him, but Wood pushed the technique the furthest in detail and furthest under the public nose.

To summarize Wood's beliefs, the fly must fish close to the surface when the air is warmer than the water, and it must cross the fish slowly at a correct broadside angle. This means that the line must float, be mended and be thoroughly controlled as it is fished and that the hooking procedure should be left to the power of the current as much as possible. Wood simplified both the number and the dressing of fly patterns until he was quite happy to fish with just three types of differing sizes, all sparsely dressed. He tried to see the fish and the take, and he likened the game to super nymphing with lighter rods, line and a far greater delicacy than every known before in the salmon world.

Wood was rich, privileged, dogmatic and enjoyed a prolific beat, fished from expertly managed banks, and many of his beliefs have

Arthur Oglesby (right) stands talking to his great friend Jim Deterding – both magnificent salmon anglers. On the right, Shirley Deterding relaxes. She is one of the country's best-known sportswomen.

been challenged because of these advantages. His square and even upstream casts, the broadside approach of the fly, the importance of air temperature, the use of his 'current alone' striking technique and the frequent mending of the line have all been questioned and modified over the years. None the less, Wood brought life and feel back into a sport long-dominated by dead and lifeless tackle. Phillip Green in *New Angles on Salmon Fishing* sums up Wood's career perfectly: 'So what is now left to me and the majority of floating line fishermen today, of the greased line method as practiced and described by Mr Wood? Low water flies certainly; method of hooking partially; but principally the floating line. What a blessing it is! Every time I use it I give silent thanks to God for the life of the man who gave it to us.'

Robert Pashley

The second giant devoted his life equally to one river – the Wye – but unlike Wood, he looked for no publicity. Robert Pashley began angling on the Wye in the 1890s, fished it for half a century, and in 1936 took 678 salmon averaging sixteen pounds, but he could never be persuaded to commit his ideas to paper. His knowledge of the Wye was profound, and he kept such a silence that visitors came to watch

A very rare shot of A.H.E. Wood fishing his stretch of the Dee. He constructed the groynes that we can see here to help the fishing.

him through field-glasses, hiding behind the trees on the steep slopes of Goodrich Castle on the far bank from him. Should Pashley see observers, then his instruction was for the gillie to drop a pool to avoid them.

What is known is that this 'Napoleon of the Wye' fished the prawn with deadly precision. He believed that the salmon developed a liking for the prawn in the sea but evolved a great respect for its serrated spear, which was liable to penetrate the soft lining of their mouths. They, therefore, needed a special form of

attack, which might account for the occasions when the prawn was recovered in a much-chewed state without the angler being aware that his bait had been taken.

Pashley was under the impression that salmon swam alongside the prawn and crushed its head and body without touching the painful spear. As a result he always took half a dozen spinning prawns and half a dozen non-spinning ones. If a spinning prawn returned in a mess, he would replace it with a non-spinning one. Very often this would be taken at the same

A magnificent catch of Wye salmon for Robert Pashley – normal, I suppose, by his standards.

spot. His belief was that the original salmon was more willing to take a dead-looking prawn as it floated past than one that could inflict severe injury on its mouth. Once the prawn was taken, Pashley watched the slight curve in the line where it entered the water, and when this curve straightened out, he struck immediately, without waiting for any pull to materialize.

Pashley began fishing the Wye when H. C. Hatton of Hereford was carrying out his experiments with the light minnow. Pashley himself gave up using heavy metal minnows and adopted Hatton's blue-and-silver and brown-and-gold ones, as well as others painted especially to his own requirements. He came

to have very definite views on the minnow and demanded a harmony of shape, size, weight and colour. He stipulated specially strengthened hooks and fins large enough to spin the bait at a fair speed but not so big that they blanked off the hook. Somehow, too, he devised a strike to draw the hook into the salmon's mouth and at the same time pull away the body of the minnow.

It was, however, Pashley's way with the fly that was most impressive. His tackle and his methods were the result of experience built up over decades of successful fishing and were put together with cold logic. Once hooked, the salmon hardly ever got away from him for he held it tight and made it do all the work close to the boat. His tackle was only a little stronger than that used by chalk stream anglers and consisted of an eleven-foot Hardy Cane Perfection rod, which was eventually changed for a steel rod of about the same length. He used a simple trout line and leaders of five- to seven-pound breaking strain. Pashley suffered badly from arthritis. His bad hip made fishing from a punt essential, and the punt was always poled by his gillie, Jack Whittingham. The two men had a vast and intimate knowledge of the pools, and Whittingham could move Pashley into exactly the right position very close to his fish. This meant that Pashley had complete control over his tackle and was constantly fishing on a short line.

RETURNING FISH

Falkus vs Profumo

In the early 1990s Hugh Falkus stirred up a great debate in the weekend *Telegraph* with a hard-hitting article that attacked the practice of returning any game fish whatsoever. The Falkus doctrine was that fishermen are hunters, not sportsmen, and that they cast a fly, a spinner or a bait in order to secure meals, not simple thrills. He said that this stance was a much more reliable one than any other against the saboteurs who still threaten the sport. If, he said, it could be proved that we were simply catching fish for our mere enjoyment and nothing else, then our stance was indefensible.

It is easy to see how Falkus adopted this view. Indeed, to some extent, he is in the old school of fishermen, brought up in straightened circumstances when anything from the wild could be a useful addition to the pot. In all his dealings with wildlife, Falkus has seen himself as a hunter as well as a conservationist, and both elements he has obviously put firmly above sport. It is an appealing doctrine that won him many friends when the debate raged, and it certainly needed to be answered.

The man who undertook the brunt of this challenge was David Profumo who answered the Falkus piece the following week. The line that Profumo took was that salmon and sea trout are simply too highly pressured in this day and age for every one to be killed, regardless of its condition, the bag, the water or any other factors. Profumo also argued that to insist on killing all game fish would drive great wedges between the game fisherman and the coarse fisherman: the latter in Britain is almost forced to return his catch. Otherwise, carefully built-up fisheries would be destroyed within a season. Any gaps opening up within the ranks of angling could be easily exploited by the saboteurs to great effect. Indeed, the whole tone of Profumo's article was for moderation and against any wild generalizations: each case really has to be looked at on its merits.

It is easy to sympathize with a great deal of what Falkus said, but at the same time there are many other considerations to bear in mind, and the flood of letters that followed seemed to confirm this. Obviously, every angler accepts that to kill a kelt (a salmon trying to return to the seas after having spawned) is wrong, even though inexperienced anglers can do this by mistake. Well-mended kelts are often difficult to pick out, and they have fooled many people in the spring. Also, most anglers would now agree that back-end fish should be treated with great respect. In many people's eyes, hen fish should go back as unharmed as possible from September onwards. Anyway, big red cock fish are hardly any gourmet's delight and can be returned without any great loss to the table.

The Argument for Release

So far, so good. Few people would disagree with this much. The question becomes more involved when fresh fish are being discussed. Surely the day of big bags being taken from the river should be a thing of the past. I well remember David Clarke of the Atlantic Salmon Trust enraged by a photograph in one of the angling magazines of two men standing over a catch of some thirty or forty salmon lying dead on the boards of their boats. His point was

David Clarke is probably one of our finest fighters for the welfare of the salmon.

that the case of the Atlantic Salmon Trust was fatally weakened in their representations to governments if anglers could be seen as such rapacious trawlers themselves! Thus, perhaps it does make sense to exercise restraint, even when the fish are silver, and the runs are prolific. Perhaps one fish taken each day is enough, or five, say, for the week. Providing the salmon is unhooked in the water by the bank rather than taken ashore, there should be no danger to its welfare in returning, and the shock of the fight should certainly not stop it ascending the river to fulfil its natural purpose.

Indeed, there have been notable experiments around the catch and release concept, most notably on the River Ewe in Wester Ross. There, the rules stated that all fish must be returned. It is worth noting that the demand for tickets on this beautiful river remained as high as before, and surely this proves that many anglers catch salmon simply for the sport and not the money or the freezer.

I suppose, in the end, there is no absolute right or wrong in this debate, and as in most controversies, there are elements of right on both sides. It should be a matter for the individual's conscience.

DAMAGE

One spring, the manager of a big salmon farm in the glen had a problem: his nets far out in the loch were being attacked on a nightly basis. The mesh was being ripped just before the water line, and tens of thousands of smolts were being lost. The financial damage was proving crippling. It was estimated that close to a million pounds worth of young salmon had been lost. Just as serious was the possibility of environmental damage. A flood of man-made six-inch fish could pose complex and far reaching problems on any delicate river system.

My poor friend was beside himself. Night after night he sat out on the loch, in the cold, with torch, binoculars and rifle. Sometimes he saw eyes on the bank. Sometimes he saw shapes in the water and even on the cages themselves, but he could not catch, kill or identify the creatures responsible. All he could say was that they descended in numbers from the southern hillside and were active principally after darkness.

We bought him a beer, sympathized, and at 10.00 p.m. we decided to go out with him – all four of us in the same boat. It was a cold night and a slight breeze picked up off the water, chilling us with its dampness. This was all the more painful as we had been softened by the crackling bar fire.

We moored by the cages and inspected the traps that had been set: they were untouched. We played a big torch on the water, and there was nothing there. However, the shoreline was pin-pricked by twenty or more pairs of eyes, reflecting the beam back to us. The creatures were waiting. For half a hour we bobbed on the water, and watched and waited, fingering the rifles. It was total stalemate, and we pulled on a flask of Grouse and discussed the problem. Pine martens or otters seemed to be the culprits, but does either species group into gangs like marauders from the Wildwood? Do pine martens swim by choice if other food is available? Anyway, both species are protected from shooting and unlawful killing. Altogether, it was not a happy crew that night.

'If they won't come to us, then we'll go to them', said Gordon finally, and we motored for the shoreline. The faces vanished, but the droppings the animals had left didn't. Still fresh and steaming from the cold night, we scooped a few into a bait box and motored back across the loch and back to the bar. Coals were heaped

A mink trapped at last.

onto the fire, the glasses were refilled and the Collins book *Tracks and Signs* was retrieved from the lounge book shelf. It was as I had thought: the droppings were without doubt from mink, probably gathered into a huge scouting party to feed the young being born in the vast forest away to the south. Mink are a real threat to squirrels, to all nestlings, to trout in the brooks and to returning salmon so vulnerable on the redds. Mink then were our culprits, a new and frightening scourge of Highland fishing.

SALMON AND WOMEN

Georgina Ballantine

A very important date in the annals of British game fishing is 7 October 1922, for on that day a woman caught a sixty-four-pound salmon from the River Tay and set a record that has lasted for approaching seventy years. Miss Georgina Ballantine was born, lived and died in a cottage only a good cast from the pool above Caputh Bridge, near Murthly, where she fought this extraordinary fish. Her father had taught her all the skills, and as Registrar in that area and friend to the local land owner Sir Alexander Lyle, he could introduce his daughter to some excellent salmon beats.

It was a Saturday and late in the afternoon when Miss Ballantine began to fish with a small natural dace (very probably a two-inch dace) on her line. Darkness was pulling in for autumn was well under way. Indeed, her father had just looked at his watch and said it was nearly time to leave when the salmon took hold. The time was exactly 6.15 p.m.

For a while, the fish moved slowly downriver, tempting Mr Ballantine to land the boat to beach the fish from the bank. Once ashore, however, Miss Ballantine knew she had a fight on her hands. In a surging two-hundred-yard run the salmon went down through Caputh Bridge, cutting Georgina's fingers as she bravely tried to slow the line down. Luckily the salmon passed through the near-side arch of the bridge, and she was able to stumble after him along the shore or there would be no story today.

It was nearly dark, and the salmon continued its downriver journey, slower it is true, but still with such inexorable power that Mr Ballantine returned for the boat so that they could follow it – all night if need be. By now, Miss Ballantine was calling the fish the 'Beast' and was quite obviously feeling the strain of the battle. She pleaded with her father to take the rod from her aching arms, but he rightly refused. Always a believer in strict fishing discipline, we are told, he would force his daughter to complete the job she had begun.

At that stage, without the boat, the fish would have been lost, for it took off irresistibly to the other side of the river, towards an island a quarter of a mile downstream. All the Ballantines could do was to follow the fleeing fish over the darkening Tay. Once again, they landed on the island above the Burnbane Pool, and though there was no light to see the salmon by, by the arch in the rod and the angle of the line they knew it was close to them now. Mr Ballantine felt along the line until he came to the swivel. He knew the length of the cast beneath, estimated the position of the fish and took the risk to gaff the salmon unseen. His judgement was unerring. The time now was 8.20 p.m., and the fight had been played out

Miss Ballantine and her father with the monster, soon after it was landed.

RECORD TAY SALMON
64 lbs
Length 54 ins Girth 25 ins
Caught on Glendelvine Water by Miss Ballantine
with Malloch Reel and Tackle
7th October 1922.

The lady and the fish. This is a studio shot and one that I do not like quite as much, even though it is obviously of better quality. It was very usual for a big fish to be taken to the studio around this time.

over half a mile of the River Tay. The fish was only slightly pink along its flanks and still had traces of sea lice, so it was a true fresh-run October giant and no stale spring fish.

This much is known to everyone, but perhaps only women can understand the full significance of that snap of an Atlantic salmon's jaws. Of course men acknowledge Miss Ballantine's achievement, but they tend to pass it by or dismiss it as just one of those things in the history of the sport. Women know better; the capture was fated and was not luck in any way. Miss Ballantine hooked the fish, played it throughout and in every way deserved to land it. Moreover, the capture of that one salmon has meant that for by far the greater part of

the twentieth century a woman has landed the biggest authenticated British freshwater fish. Every ounce of its sixty-four-pound frame speaks of glory, muscle and power – and it capitulated to a woman only a little larger than itself. If you are lucky enough to see a cast of the fish, it is a revelation. The fish is simply huge, with scales and fins such as you have never seen before.

Lady Game Anglers

There are many excellent women anglers, especially in the game world. Many of these ladies are fortunate to have been born to or married into wealth and position and have exploited it in angling terms to the full. There are few better salmon anglers than Her Majesty The Queen Mother who over the years has caught many salmon with grace and skill, but she is far from being alone. For example, in 1924 Mrs Morrison took a fly-caught fifty-one-pound salmon on the Deveron. In 1923 Miss Doreen Davey took a fish of fifty-nine pounds eight ounces from the Wye, and a little earlier a Miss Radclyffe accounted for two fish of over forty pounds in two days on the Tay (both were caught on the fly).

In 1935 Lady Joan Joicey, spinning in the Tweed in February, killed twenty-six salmon and two sea trout during a single day's fishing. In 1930 Mrs Barbara Williams caught two Wye salmon on consecutive days which weighed between them eighty-six pounds! Like Miss Ballantine, she too had a fishing father – a Mr Wyndham-Smith who once took a brace of fish from the Wye within half an hour of each other that weighed a staggering ninety-four pounds. There cannot have been many double catches any greater within a single family.

Today, there are other successful lady game anglers. I know that Grace Oglesby, wife of the very famous author, catches a good number of fish, as does her great sporting friend from Norfolk, Shirley Deterding. Other notable ladies to add to this list are Mrs Hugh Blakeney and Francis Shand-Kydd.

For several years, I stayed at the Tilmouth Park Hotel on the Tweed, and once I was fortunate enough to watch the owner of the hotel and the estate, Lady David Burnett, cast for, hook and play a large salmon. My vantage point was a cliff face twenty yards above the river. Every action that was carried out beneath me was neat, precise and utterly controlled. The fact that Lady Burnett lost the fish at the net was simple misfortune and detracted nothing from her legend as far as I was concerned. Certainly, the hallway of that famous and excellent hotel bore testimony to her skill in the past: the cast of an enormous salmon caught by that excellent fishing lady looked down on every visitor that entered.

Are Women Better Anglers?

I have heard the secret of such ladies' successes explained away by their willingness to listen to the advice of their gillies and carry it out to the letter. It is argued that ladies are denied the experience that male anglers build up over a lifetime's fishing. As a result, they simply and sensibly use the props provided for them. Whatever the gillie says, the lady angler does, and she is therefore sometimes more successful than the male angler who goes his own pig-headed way. I am sure that this theory is over-simplistic.

At the other extreme, research was recently carried out hoping to prove that women are better salmon anglers than men. This was attributed to something in their genes, their vibrations, their psyche, their scent or their pheromones (whatever they are) that prompts a response from salmon. It was seriously suggested that in some way the salmon, the fresh-run fish anyway, identifies better with a female than a male. I just cannot see the truth in this. We have to consider the fact that most of the hooks that caught the lengendary big fish for women over the years were tied to the line by very masculine gillies.

Perhaps it is something to do with casting. Women frequently have more rhythm and better timing than men and can throw a better line. The Honourable Mrs Hooper, sister of Lord Glanusk, proved to be an excellent salmon fly caster during the early part of the twentieth century. On the Usk, in the 1930s a Miss Mary Dawson was a disciple of the tackle shop owner and casting champion Lionel Sweet, and she proved herself successful at many competitions. Certainly, in the 1920s and 1930s, women frequently dominated the casting arenas, achieving distances beyond men's capabilities, despite the obvious disadvantages of less natural strength and body muscle.

The Importance of Wealth

Wealth, surely, is a very important part of any discussion about salmon and women anglers. Why there are so few lady coarse anglers did once mystify me. With typical chauvinism, I put it down to the feminine dislike of maggots and worms, to their sensitivity to the cold or their dislike of mud, slime and general discomfort. Then the penny dropped: women work harder than men – perhaps not always on a nine-to-five basis, but in the home, which is a constant chore. A lady can go salmon fishing a few times – even twenty times – a year, with her husband, on holiday, but to accompany him once or twice a week for eight or fourteen hours a day every month of the season would be next to impossible. Whilst it has long been accepted that the husband, the male coarse angler, has Sunday at the very least by the waterside, it has rarely been possible for his wife to leave the children, ignore the meal times and desert the home on such a regular time-consuming basis. Should she work as well, then the problem is compounded. Never has it been accepted that the family woman has the right to time called her own.

The situation has been historically different for ladies of the upper-middle and upper classes. Throughout the nineteenth century and right into the mid-twentieth century at least, more money, more leisure time, more freedom of travel and far greater help in the home bestowed more freedoms on ladies of sufficiently independent spirit to seize them.

GLENGARRY SALMON TRAPS

Many years ago, by Act of Parliament, salmon traps were placed across the upper Glengarry River so that salmon could be caught, stripped, their eggs hatched, and the resulting parr released back into the river system. It was a

far-sighted and extravagant attempt to improve the runs of fish in a river that had suffered from hydro-electric schemes. During certain years, the traps certainly seemed to prove effective.

For several days, the temperature had been dropping over north-west Scotland. Frosts had become severe, and snow had fallen for several hours each day so that the tops of the Munroes had a thick white coat, and even the lower glen had a fair covering. The flakes had cooled and raised the river, and now the salmon just had to make their last push to the fish traps

On the way to the fish traps.

placed high in the system. Each morning the fishery men checked the traps, found them empty and went away puzzled and disappointed, but on one particular Wednesday all this changed quite suddenly.

The twin iron cages across the river simply pulsated with salmon – big and small, red and silver, cock and hen. Reinforcements were radioed for, and they arrived in a van from the nearest town. Throughout the day the salmon were netted, emptied into buckets and taken to the huge tanks by the river fed by a plume of water from an eight-inch-diameter pipe. By the time the sun began to sink behind Gairich, fifty-four males and twenty-three females had been captured and counted, all fish that had swum up during the previous night.

There were spectacular surprises that astonished even the hardened fishery workers. There was a near thirty-pound cock, four feet of scarlet marble, swimming next to a hen of similar size but still as silver as the icicles hanging around the river bank. There was a four-pound grilse, complete with spinner in its jaws and broken fifteen-pound line (explain that if you can). There was a big female pike weighing perhaps fifteen pounds that had ghosted into the cage attracted by all the movement and the promise of food. Finally, and almost best of all, there was a magnificent fourteen-pound ferox trout that made everybody there that day feel that something quite special had happened before their very eyes.

The trapped fish milled around in the tanks, and as the short Highland day petered out, the fishery men left to get back to the Great Glen before dark and snowstorms set in once again. Stripping the salmon could begin another day. My journey was only a mile or two to the Tomdoun Hotel, so I stayed a while, happy to hear the stags roaring in the corries and see the moon glow over the mountain tops and glitter on the river. How glad I am that I lingered on.

An otter crossed the silver river. It had watched the day's proceedings from a holt beneath some birch trees, and now it knew to come and reap a rich reward for observation

and patience. There were some big wire frames lying on the ground, and I put these over the tanks. That put paid to his supper plans, and he watched me with almost visible disdain before disappearing off eastwards towards Loch Poulary.

Still I stayed, though it was now seven and I could smell a lavish dinner in my imagination. All the while the fish in the tank by me had been becoming more and more restless, and when the moon shone out again on them I could see them chasing around their prison, topping, gulping in air. Then something quite extraordinary began. Fish after fish approached the solid eight-inch torrent of water from the tap, and one after another, time after time, tried to climb it. Some reached the tap itself, their heads actually forcing into the metal cavity before being swept back to their comrades beneath. I held my own hand in the flow from the tap, but the force of the water was so great that I could not keep it there more than a second or two. The sight was enough to make anybody's heart bleed. These brave fish, so impelled by nature to attempt the impossible, continued their hopeless journey throughout the coming seventeen-hour night.

HEROES: THE FISHING DANE

Borge Munk Jensen is a lesson to us all and an example of how a love for salmon and for fishing in general can keep any man young. Borge is now in his late seventies and is probably the best-known angling writer in Denmark. I met him for the first time in 1993 in Copenhagen airport and was to spend the next two weeks in his company, often in the most trying of environments. However, I never heard a single word of complaint from him. This particular trip was around his 170th major international fishing excursion, and listening to him during interminable stop-overs at Russian airports was an education. It did not matter what country, what river or what fish species you mentioned,

My great friend and a fine fish.

Borge had been there and done it. Not that he bragged in any way: he simply sat over a cup of coffee and in his quiet way explained exactly the problems that would face a man on such a journey. If one simply mentioned fish or fishing, his whole face took on a totally new and animated look. Actually, I thought Borge was in his sixties and, as you can see, I was almost twenty years out.

After thirty-six hours of strenuous travelling, we arrived at a houseboat in a bay off the Caspian Sea. I and the other much younger members of the party were shattered and wanted to sleep, but not Borge. Life is too short to sleep when you can be out with a fishing rod in your hand; I know that now, thanks to him. All those

days it was Borge who was first up, first into the boats, first to be fishing and last to want to stop. His stamina and his will-power were equally stunning, and he just never seemed to tire of the fascinating job in hand. This was made even more remarkable by the species of fish that we were catching: beluga sturgeon. These are massive fish, averaging two hundred pounds and frequently going far bigger than that.

We hooked and lost fish well into four figures. Every battle was a back-breaking experience and to bring a beluga to a boat in under an hour was exceptional. There was no rest during any of the fights either. Beluga are big wild fish, hooked in very strong turbulent rivers, and often the first runs will take two hundred yards of line off the reel. Pumping fish like these back is desperate work, but Borge did it again and again, day after day. He was always happy, always laughing, always talking fishing, always revelling in a new experience in this exotic Caspian landscape.

However, this is a salmon book and it is as a salmon hero that Borge takes his place. Every year for half a century Borge has visited Norway, and his salmon successes up there have caused sensations round Scandinavia. I am not surprised, for having seen Borge fish, I know that he works with intensity and passion as well as skill, and the combination of all these things is irresistible. At Christmas 1993, he sent me a card featuring himself and his wife and a beautiful Norwegian springer. It took pride of place on my mantelpiece, and I was proud to think that such a great fisherman should remember me.

HEROES: MACASKILL OF INVERGARRY

It was in the late 1980s that I first knocked on his door, at the end of a spring snowstorm that laid a coating over the bank of the River Garry, obliterating, for a while, the carpet of flowers. An old bicycle was leaning against the wall, so I knew that he was in. I knocked again, to make myself heard above the roar of the river. The handle turned, and an elderly man peered out at me, blinking in the bright light. He ushered me into a small, dark sitting room where a fire burned noisily. He asked what he could do for me. I was fully aware of my temerity. Jock MacAskill's uncertain temper was well known through the glen, and I was told I might receive a barbed reception – especially as I was enquiring about pike rather than the lordly salmon. My forebodings could not have been more misplaced. Jock was the absolute soul of generosity.

He told me one or two extraordinary tales that day, making my decision to leave the loch seem ever more the correct one. First, he dealt

This is not Jock himself, but he has the look about his eyes of an old Norfolk gillie.

with my query about pike on the River Garry system. I say 'dealt', but really he blew my mind! It seems that in the years just after the War he laid nets down here and there in the shallows, at spawning time, to see if he could make any inroads into the pike population. It was some time during the 1950s that he pulled his nets in one fateful day and found a fifty-one-pound female pike. Of course, he did not think to photograph the fish: what on earth could it really mean to fanatical salmon fishermen apart from a parr- or even grilse-eater? However, Jock, being the true sportsman, saw the light in my eyes and heard the enthusiasm in my voice and told me everything he could about the fish.

Then we moved on to salmon. He took out

a wallet of black-and-white photographs that would have stunned any salmon fisher, no matter how experienced, no matter where he had fished or in what age. These were Jock's trophies of the River Garry before the hydro-electric schemes. There was photograph after photograph of Jock, his fishermen and his fish – vast springers, lying on the snow, gleaming in the summer sunshine or resplendent in autumn colours. Jock told me he had lost count of the number of big fish he had caught or landed for clients, and I well believe him: I even lost count of the number of photographs he showed me, but I wish to goodness now that I had had the sense to take copies that day.

I stayed with Jock at Garry bank all that afternoon and on into the evening when we decided to cross the river into the inn by the bridge. Soon the night took on an unreal atmosphere, and I still treasure an image of Jock talking to me about his ancestors, his fishing and his life. Jock was one of eight children, and his mother was related to the former lairds of Glengarry who controlled all the land west as far as Knoydart. In fact, he told me his ancestors had been traced back to the royal houses of Scotland in the eighth century. I realized how proud Jock was of this fabulous lineage. At times, as the hours drifted and the whisky intake increased, he lapsed into the native Gaelic and completely lost me.

Apart from the war years, Jock had been a gillie from 1923 until 1986, and probably no man in Scotland could claim a greater knowledge of his own particular river than he could of the Garry. After that first meeting, I made a point of seeing Jock before anybody else in the glen whenever I arrived. He would always tell me exactly where I stood the best chance of salmon, trout, char or pike, and his advice was always absolutely and immediately correct. During the next few years I heard more and more stories about Jock, his stalking abilities, his fishing captures, his wild sense of humour and the scrapes he would get himself into late at night after too much whisky. I saw him a good few times in his kilt and finery, proud as

a pigeon and ready for a song or a story or a scotch! One of the happiest nights was when I was called upon to take a photograph of him, his son and his grandson. The two younger MacAskills had been trolling in Loch Garry when the grandson's rod hooped round and he played a near ten-pound ferox to the boat – just about as many pounds as the boy was in years! The fish was brought from the hotel larder and a gasp went round the bar. The three men gathered round the fireplace under stuffed fish and historic photographs and cradled the fish between them. It was hard to know which of the three was the prouder, and I knew when I clicked the shutter I was taking a photograph of historic importance.

On 13 November 1992, the telephone rang, and an old friend was on the line. It appeared that the day before, Jock was killed, tragically, in a car accident close to his home village. I still regret not being able to get north for his funeral, which I was told was a moving Highland affair, with pipers and drams at the churchyard gate. It was as though the whole of Glengarry, Knoydart and even the north-west of Scotland was there, with a line of mourners two miles long leading to the cemetery. That is hard to believe knowing how few people inhabit those remote parts, but then I guess Jock was so special that every single one of them must have made an effort to turn up and see him off. Glengarry is now a poorer place for everybody.

SURVIVING ON THE CATCH

There are still remote Highland rivers that offer salmon fishing of the old sort that existed before roads were put down and fishing huts became palaces. In these places, the best pools are approached by trails over the hills made by anglers, deer or stalking ponies. Sometimes the distances are so great that it is best to spend the night in an outlying bothy. If the night is still, and if it is mild, you simply have to pray that the hut is sound or the midges will be in, and not the most acrid pipe will drive them

There is no need for a gillie when travelling light in wild places.

out. Your bed will be an old bench perhaps, but this is good enough because you will be exhausted and able to sleep on anything. Dinner could well be left-overs from lunch – unless you actually have a salmon with you, and then a real celebration is quite possible.

I was in Kashmir when a particular way of cooking fish at a campfire was shown to me. We had been fishing the River Lidder and had gone so far up the valley that the night caught us totally unawares. There was nothing my guide and I could do but settle on a sandy beach by our last pool and prepare for the night. I freely admit that I was very hungry and moaned a good deal to my Kashmiri guide, who seemed to take the whole situation well in his stride. 'No problem' was all he would say.

The sky was brilliantly lit with stars as we rooted around in the light jungle looking for firewood left by marauding parties from the nearest village. Soon, however, we had a merry little blaze crackling away, giving warmth in a night that was rapidly becoming chilly. The guide took two of the trout that we had caught right at the end of the day, gutted them and wrapped them in wet newspaper. He waited until the fire was going well and some hot embers had been produced. Then, using a stick, he buried the parcels of trout and left them for around fifteen minutes, occasionally turning them over or pushing them further into the embers.

At last he inspected one carefully and pronounced that the trout were ready. I waited for the paper to cool and unwrapped it. As the paper fell away so did the skin from the fish, leaving perfectly cooked, succulent flesh to be devoured . . . and it was!

Nothing could be simpler, and it is the type of recipe even a fool like me can follow. It is very rare that you will find a bothy without some old newspapers stacked somewhere if you have not had the foresight to bring your own, and, of course, water is rarely a problem!

Actually, I prefer to eat any salmon cooked by this method cold. Cook it and leave it in the paper whilst you go and have a last cast or two in the darkening pools, unless the midges are too bad. When you return, the salmon should have cooled, and the flesh will be as moist as a morning mist and you will be glad to have missed some dry old stuff down the valley in the hotel.

GILLIES

Gillies can be quite awe-inspiring characters, as they were to Charles Kingsley, author of the *Water Babies*: '. . . the river god in coat of velveteen, elbow on knee and pipe in mouth'. Every game fisherman has his memories of a favourite gillie on a favourite beat, from a special week or so of life. The number of gillies today looks like rising again. As bodies like the Atlantic Salmon Trust buy the nets off the rivers, the salmon runs strengthen, numbers of anglers increase and the one-time netsmen become smartly dressed gillies themselves. On whom should these new gillies model themselves?

The Ideal Gillie?

According to the late Terry Thomas, it would be Bill Law, the man known as the best gillie in Scotland. Bill combined many gifts. He was a great salmon and trout angler, and he was an exceptionally successful tournament caster. Terry remembered him using a Malloch reel in the bait accuracy event at Crystal Palace in 1935, changing the spool angle so quickly, one could scarcely see what he was doing. A good gillie also knows his river and its flies, and Bill was a first-class practical entomologist and a fly dresser who bred his own fowl for their hackles. Bill also knew the river and its valley in all the various moods. Once, observing that a storm in the mountains was causing the river to rise, Bill grabbed Terry by the arm and ran him half a mile upstream to a spot where he had two salmon in the space of a few minutes.

Terry saw in Bill Law the self-taught pragmatism that was possessed by William Lumm. Both, he said, went for the obvious. Bill always wore army ammunition boots instead of canvas waders because on some of the stretches he fished they gave more ankle support, preventing strains or breaks. The relationship between Terry and Bill is very typical of that between many a salmon man and his gillie. As Terry said, 'Bill knew me as a small boy. I shot my first rabbits with him – 'shoot them in the lugs!', he said. I caught my first sea trout with him. But he did not pass on his wisdom easily. It took years and a world war before, in a series of stages, I worked out his logical, obvious approach. Bill did not only keep his cards close to his chest, but he kept them there for a long time.'

This was Bill Law, just one of a brave line of gillies. These are men of the waterside who know their rivers, their flies, their fish and all the natural world that surrounds them. They can be gruff and forbidding, but beneath that they are kindly and often take young anglers firmly under their capacious wings. They are brave men who will see off poachers and support the good of the river, come what may. Very many of them are characters.

The 'King of the Glen'

Take, for example, a certain Hector A. Mac-Donald who was the absolute king of the glens. He lived at the Tomdoun when the hotel was a farm, a garage, a post office and a telephone exchange as well as a place to stay. As I once wrote, he was the prince of the whole team of gillies who served the sportsmen of the early and mid-century. Then, only paying guests entered through the front doors of the hotel, and the grooms, the glen men and the gillies all used the rough bar that is still in part standing at the rear of the hotel, among the bothies, sheds and stores. There, night after night, season after season, Hector A. MacDonald held sway.

Every salmon lie, every hill lochan, every twist of the burns and every drop away in the lochs he knew intimately. He was a beautiful caster, a crack shot and a strong oarsman. He was the personification of sport in the glen and often had scant respect for those who employed him. He could be truculent, and he invariably took credit for any capture. It was said you shouldn't trust him with a bottle or with a girl, but he was always forgiven and revered for his knowledge and love of the glen. Nothing, it seemed, would ever keep him away from it.

The war came, and Hector's shooting skill was needed. He was captured and sent to work in a Silesian mine. There, he eventually feigned blindness. The Germans put him through countless tests, often painful, and he never flinched. Finally, defeated, they shipped him home and he landed at Southampton, still 'blind'. The government of the day took him back to his glen and gave him a pension for life. However, once the bureaucrats' backs were turned, Hector, blind as an eagle, continued his work as before! To the end of his days, Hector could see 'a dram on a mountain top five miles away'. Nothing could or would keep Hector from his life's love.

The Gillie and the Angler

I don't know if it is possible to lay down rules about gillies, as there are so many different

A gillie has always provided a shoulder to lean upon and sound advice in a crisis.

characters, and after all we are dealing with very sensitive human beings here! Of course, the standard of gillies varies greatly: some see themselves as little more than oarsmen for the day, whilst others make themselves indispensable. It really does make sense to listen to what the gillie says to you.

If you are not an expert, do not pretend to be. A gillie can assess an angler's ability by his tackle, his address, his approach to the water and his very first cast. Name-dropping and airs and graces will not impress him. Make suggestions, if you want, once you know the man and the water. Once there is a bond between you, your own original thinking will be admired, discussed and possibly adopted.

Very often a gillie's ways will be strange to you, but it is still wise to listen and go along with them, at least at the start. I remember Arthur Oglesby talking about the use of the gaff with virtually all Norwegian salmon. To Arthur (as to most of us) the gaff is an unnecessary instrument, but as he said Norwegian salmon are something out of most anglers' normal ken, and so large are they that netting or tailing would be a risky business. This excellent angler's approach is obviously the correct one: 'I would be doing my host a disservice and a discourtesy if I, arrogantly, threw Norwegian tradition to one side, ordered my gillie out of the way, and attempted to get the fish out my own way'. You just have to listen and do things the traditional way of the river.

Treat a gillie as you would like to be treated. Would you want to be kept out in the dourest weather when you know there is no chance of a fish, to be blamed for things out of your own control or to be left with absolutely all the physical work to do? Remember a gillie is there to try and help you catch fish and should not be regarded as some beast of burden. Some gillies like to eat their lunch a little way off, and so it might be with yours. Offer hospitality, please, but do not force it on the poor man who wants a bit of quiet, a smoke or some contemplation on his own. A few pounds does not buy a man body and soul after all.

I've spent a good deal of words on gillies simply because they are so central to the catching of fish, especially on rivers strange to you. More than that, they are vital to the enjoyment of the day and to an understanding of the river. A good gillie, on your side, cannot do the impossible, but he will do his level best, which comes very close in many cases.

A LITTLE DIVERSIFICATION

The scene is the Tillmouth Park Hotel. It is late summer/early autumn back in the early 1980s. All the residents were on the boats out on the very slack Tweed. Anglers and water were tired and despondent. No one went out until mid-morning, and all were back early in the afternoon, for on a river so low spirits just seemed to die away. Some even paid their bills and travelled southwards. Those that remained had no current to work a fly in and no depth and far too much weed for a spinner. Occasional salmon were seen, but the majority had been long in the river and were so reddened that you could only feel sorry for them. In short, here was a fishing hotel in despondency.

The big spates were only days or weeks off, and then fresh salmon would run against the surge of water. All the beats were booked, all the boats taken, and the hotel was full of anticipation for coming big fish. As for now, the gillies would have rather been off the river, working on their boats, seeing to their vegetable gardens.

I went my own way, leaving the heavy tackle and taking up a light trout rod, walking towards the lower Till where nothing would restrict me. If there is any place in the world that God created in the fashion of heaven itself, then it is surely that point where these two rivers meet. They join behind a great island that shelters the scene from savage north winds, and they are overlooked by the remains of a chapel that was built in His honour, in the wilds, away from any habitation, on those last few yards of English soil.

If Salmon Fishing Fails . . .

God (many salmon anglers hardly appreciate this fact) also created grayling, and there they found their own paradise, on the bend of this lovely junction, just where the mighty stream met the smaller one and the gracefully weeping trees.

All that period, I was alone there. The sandy beach had no footprints, the fisherman's hut was secured, and the padlock lay rusted, unused in the loneliness of that place. A misty afternoon was merging with dusk, and in no more than half-light, I knelt on the sand bar and cast to the point where the Till ran out rapidly over a long gravel bar before delving into the larger river. It was as long a cast as I could easily make, upstream, but sweeping down opposite and finally beneath me, the line moving like the second hand of an enormous watch face.

When it had reached the one o'clock mark, I had the feeling that the fly was not alone in the world any longer – for a change! I felt no tug, no take. The line did not halt or move upstream, and there was no sensation through the rod. I did not know. I was not sure. On the second cast I was more careful to lay down a wisp of line, and once again the rod began to tingle for me. There was no gleam in the water, no bulge. In fact, there was nothing more than a fantasy in the twilight. Soon the valley was too dark and wet to continue, and I strayed homewards.

I was the only angler in the hotel that night who looked forward to the following day because I was the only one with a secret, with a challenge facing, with any real prospect of success ahead of me. Nagging doubts had chased me all along the valley to the hotel. I wondered if the fish I imagined were only cheating bits of weed whose duplicity would be revealed by the next morning's daylight. However, deep down, I knew the species I had brushed with was grayling, and I was very excited. I knew that my hopes of grayling would excite interest or enthusiasm in very few of the salmon-seeking bar grumblers, so I kept my find quiet.

Next morning, the dew lay in an unbroken sheen along the path, and flights of duck rose up in curtains as I approached. The rabbits could hardly believe their startled eyes. Where the fir tree pressed in, I tore the silver-beaded spider webs, and where the valley widened out, I frightened off the heron wading beneath the railway bridge.

My first cast of the new day snaked out, and as before bellied with the flow. I watched the leader along every knot over every boulder with a burning desire for action. It came so fast, so dramatically, that the take of the fish could be heard as it slashed the tight line through the water. Everybody knows that magic when a fish is on, and all one can do is give slack to a fleeing devil.

The fish was plunging, revolving onto its back, gleaming its slim yellow belly, hanging in the current, harrowing away in short thrusts and rattling the rod tip. Yard by yard, I worked it into the shallows, where it swam higher in the water, where the proud dorsal of the big grayling extended. I could watch the fish in the now-sunlit clear water, her fins erect, her gills flaring, her whole body working as she fought the thin strand of nylon.

Yes, all right, this fish was only about one-tenth as big as a salmon, but she was beautiful all the same. Her pectoral and ventral fins were gold and yellow, and the latter were marbled with brown over the gold, looking like the breast of a thrush caught in a shaft of sunlight. Her eye was ringed deep with gold. Most beautiful were the top three rows of scales from her head to her tail, which now caught the light from the sky then the reflections from the water and glistened in turn with shifting silvers, blues and purples. Strangely, on each flank, parallel to each other from the head to the ventral fin, ran two golden lines as if traced in gold dust by some angel. I was looking at colours that no one but an angler ever sees, that exist nowhere else in the world but on these remarkable, little-sought-after fish,

The Arctic char can make a fine addition to any basket.

colours that were caught in the netherland between water and air.

I remember just how happy I was, almost singing happy, and I compared my feelings with those of the disconsolate salmon anglers, complaining yet again over their evening meal. Salmon are magnificent – there is no doubt about that – but sometimes, when all the dice are loaded against you, it pays to have a look at what else the river holds and rescue what could otherwise be a very blank week indeed.

THIS SPORTING LIFE

A good deal of autumnal salmon fishing in the Highlands centres around the lodge or the country house party. Stalking and shooting are at their peak, and if a salmon river runs within

the estate everyone's sport is catered for. Lodges can be hired on a weekly, fortnightly or monthly basis, or leased for a season or any specified number of years. One can, of course, buy them outright.

These parties can present problems, however. For instance, often more people want to stalk than the moor can take. Perhaps nobody wants to fish because the river is too low. Alternatively, if there are fish up, then eight want rods and there are only three decent pools and four fishing outfits anyway. Breakfast can be tense to say the least!

Be Prepared

It is quite easy to be intimidated when that first invitation comes in, perhaps from somebody you half got to know on a river the previous spring and had virtually forgotten about since. It is best to explore the financial arrangements first. For example, you need to know if you are a guest or a paying guest, and if the latter how much you will be expected to contribute. If you will be paying a good deal, are you happy that the fishing, the food and even the company is worth the expense? Resentment is a killer, especially if the weather is wet, sport is poor, the rooms are cold and you have a bed over the generator that wakes you up on the hour, every hour through the night when that incontinent general stops snoring, switches on his light and marches loudly down to the corridor to relieve himself with the energy and noise of a spate river.

You can expect a lodge to be cold, for heating four state rooms, ten double bedrooms, kitchens, drying rooms and staff quarters is not cheap when the wind begins to blow the sleet at the windows. Nights can be freezing, so make sure you arrive early, choose the best room, and take the spare blanket and at least one of the two pre-war electric fires that will be hidden in the under-stairs cupboard. Moan, then, with the rest of your breakfast party, but don't let anybody into your room, or you will be undone and as cold as the rest.

Have a firm idea of how you want to spend your time, and stick to it. If you are there for salmon, then trumpet the fact, and the ditherers will both accept that and you as the expert. Do not, though, accede to all requests for loaning flies: you won't get them back, and five people losing five flies each day can get expensive.

Be wary of agreeing to teach a woman or a child to fish. It is all too easy, when the port

A typical Scottish scene: a view of a very productive salmon pool.

begins to flow and the eyes flash alluringly over the candlelight, to agree to something you will regret the next day. I know there is a thesis that women make the best salmon anglers, but there are those who show little fish sense, water sense or common sense, and I well remember finding a tube fly buried impenetrably into my skull one windy day on the Lochy. A trip to a hospital was out of the question, and I had to grin and bear it as a 'butcher' from the lodge set about me with a carving knife and a bottle of vodka for us both. Mind you, trying to teach men over the age of twenty is almost as bad. Male or female, if you don't learn to fly cast early you have to be very keen to learn and really work at it.

Social Graces

If all goes well, and you catch a salmon, be ultra careful. There will be heavy pressure on you to donate the brightest and the best of your fish to the dinner table. Your pride and your good nature might well lead you to agree, and if you are a non-paying guest you will probably be obliged to hand the fish over with the best of grace. Otherwise, do not be steamrollered: a wedding anniversary, an important birthday or a request from the Palace are all good excuses to hang on to what you have won after hours of cold, damp and frustration.

There are lots of minor things you must do: for example, don't forget to tip the cook, especially if he or she has been cheerful and long-suffering and shown any talent at all. Often they are rather exploited by the agencies that hire them out, and if you can make their lives a little bit easier, then I feel that you should.

Prepare for the dinner times. These can be hours of unbridled merriment or lifetime sentences of boredom and embarrassment. Always check up on what you'll be wearing. It is embarrassing to go down in a sports jacket to find everybody else resplendent in black tie – or even worse the other way round! Try to sit next to somebody at least half-sane, and if you

can't do that, suggest rotating after each course. Exaggerate every one of your accomplishments if you are the type that doesn't want to be overlooked. If your accomplishments are very widely known, then understate them dramatically. Both ploys will have a dramatic effect. Once you have owned up to living in any county, you will almost certainly be barraged with names of the jet/county set that lives there. You can admit to not knowing the first couple of names thrown at you, but thereafter be either hazy or positive. Try to think of the largest landowner in the county, and suggest that you think you met these particular people at one of his dinner parties. Say anything that shows you are somebody of standing.

Above all, have a joke ready. The chances are that some time around the appearance of the port, a fool will suggest jokes all round. If you can begin with a cracker, then you will be regarded with affectionate respect and let off for the rest of the stay. I am terrible at remembering jokes, and I was rescued once by an incident on the way to a lodge in Invernessshire. On the journey, just over the borders, the lady accompanying me inadvertently put her hand on a Scotsman's bare leg, just below the kilt, as we were sitting at a bar having a drink. It was thirty seconds before she realized what she had done, and she removed her hand with a scream: 'It's gruesome!'

'Put it back, lassie', the 'Old Jock' replied. 'It's just grew some more!'

SALMON AND SOCIAL HISTORY

Anybody who has done 'O' level history in the last half-century will have heard of Thomas William Coke of Holkham, a man born in 1754, and one of this country's most revered agriculturalists. It was said of Holkham before Coke took over that all you would see there would be a blade of grass and two rabbits fighting for it. However, things were soon to change.

New crops, crop rotation, better soil preparation and the introduction of new strains of sheep all transformed Holkham and Norfolk farming. Through Coke's lifetime rents from the estate rose tenfold, and every summer for forty years a gathering took place at Holkham called 'Coke's Clippings'. To this great sheep-shearing came farmers, scientists and anybody interested in agriculture from all parts of the country and abroad.

This first Coke was a countryman of simple tastes. All through his life he rose before dawn, visited the dairy and persuaded the dairyman to give him a mug of cream. Then, by tradition, he went to the bakehouse, pulled the crusty ends from the hot loaves, dipped them in the cream and made a breakfast of them. After that, he would mount his horse and ride the estate. In an age when the labouring man often lived in a leaking straw-thatched hovel in fear of unemployment and the poor house, with drunkenness his only escape from misery, Coke's people had good cottages with neat gardens and a secure future. For all these things Coke became a household name in the early-nineteenth century, as well as Leader of the House of Commons. Eventually he was created the Earl of Leicester in 1837, the first peer created by young Queen Victoria. In this way, a great aristocratic dynasty was founded. There is still a Viscount Coke at Holkham, and the estate still flourishes as it did two hundred years ago.

The Treasures of Holkham

So what? Why this ponderous history lesson? Because within the great house, designed by William Kent, you will find amongst the magnificent paintings by Rubens, Raphael, Van Dyck, Leonardo, Reynolds, Gainsborough and the rest, one of the greatest treasures any

Coke	U. Sandia.	28. 24. 25. 20.
Hamilton	L. Sandia	30. 60. 26.
Rotburghe	U. Vina.	26. 34
Corbet.	L. Vina	23. 24. 21. 30. 25. 21. 19.
Hamilton	U. Sandia.	27. 32. 24.
Coke	L. Sandia.	26. 45. 23. 28. 24. 28. 20. 21. 2
Corbet.	U. Vina.	32. 24.
Rotburghe	L. Vina	20. 22. 26. 17. 26. 27 24
Coke	U. Sandia.	16. 25. 40. 26.

A historic photograph from the Holkham Game Book. It contains sizes and numbers of fish that many would believe impossible today. (Photograph by courtesy of Visc. Coke)

A magnificent tarpon caught by one of the Earls of Leicester and now resplendent at Holkham Hall. (Photograph by courtesy of Viscount Coke)

33 pounder caught July 16th 1907

Yet another colossal fish in the Holkham collection. (Photograph by courtesy of Visc. Coke)

salmon angler could imagine. The Earl of Leicester, you see, was a mighty salmon fisherman, and there still exists at Holkham his record book, bound in white hide, meticulously kept, the big fish marked exquisitely in red. Above all, this is an historic record of the great years between 1913 and 1929 when Leicester and his group of friends made an almost annual trip to Norway's Alten River. That very first year set the tone: Leicester, Dalhousie, General Sir Redvers Buller and Colonel North Dalrymple-Hamilton fished between 28 June and 27 July and landed 172 fish for a total weight of 3,125 pounds. On the last day, Dalrymple-Hamilton took a fifty-eight-pound fish. (His personal account for that month was fifty-seven fish for 956 pounds.)

There are other treasures in the back rooms of Holkham Hall, notably collections of photo albums detailing a hundred years in the life of one of our greatest families. There are pictures of travel and domestic life, but above all of sport. Kings, princes and prime ministers are all featured there, frequently over bags of pheasant and partridge, but outnumbering even these are prints of water and fishing. It seems that almost every Coke was born with a rod in his or her hand. There are pictures of the girls practising their fly casting on the lawn in front of the house, of children standing upright and proud with their first salmon, of house parties on the Thurso and Test (favourite rivers) and, obviously, of great Alten itself.

Again, I can hear you saying so what? Why this slavish interest in the doings of the rich and the famous? I think it is important to realize that salmon has always had a special place in our sporting affections. The salmon, the pheasant and the stag have proved an enduring triumvirate that continues to attract the attention of all sportsmen. The strange thing is that a century ago – and less – salmon were not particularly expensive to fish for. Rather it was the ability of people like the Cokes to be able to travel and to take time away that was so important. Few indeed were

those able to travel to Scotland, never mind to Norway, before the 1950s or 1960s. Holidays were counted in days not weeks for ninety-nine per cent of the population, and a month beside a river was beyond the ken of all but the mighty and privileged few.

For this reason, salmon rivers were barely fished then, by comparison with nowadays. Go back forty years or so, and you would find half or even a quarter the number of rods on any given beat that you will today. Also, it is quite obvious that the Cokes and their parties only fished when the levels were right. They would not flog useless water, but rather spend the day elsewhere. This was the norm, not the exception. Today, salmon anglers fish whatever the conditions, whatever the numbers of fish present and whatever the number of anglers on the beat. Salmon fishing has for many people on most rivers changed beyond recognition.

There is one final, great mystery remaining at Holkham Hall, something of massive interest to the historians of our sport. Through the 1920s Colonel North Dalrymple-Hamilton took a 'cinema' with him and Coke to Norway – a cinematograph with which they took motion pictures of each other landing giant fish. These films tragically seem to be missing. If only they could be found we would actually be able to watch some of the greatest twentieth-century salmon anglers in action and some of the biggest fish of the century being caught in the type of world we will never quite experience again.

LINES ON THE WATER

There cannot be a more tranquil place to while away a winter's day when the rain teems down than in a salmon fisher's library, sitting in an easy chair beneath row upon row of salmon classics that stretch back over two hundred years. The spines gleam in the light from the chandelier (so dismal is the day that the lights are switched on even though it is early afternoon). The smell of after-lunch coffee drifts around the house, and the dogs snooze before the fire in the drawing-room just down the passage. It's an old country scene with an old feel. Like all good libraries, it has a grandfather clock in the corner, ticking away our lives, now as it did before the very first of the books was written.

The little library table boasts an old silver letter opener, beautifully decorated with a leaping salmon. There are pictures of fishing scenes on the wall, and best of all, through the window and down across the meadow, lies a carp lake, gloomy now beneath the tall gaunt trees of January. You know that from that lake runs a small stream that eventually enters the trout river where you will be spending so much of the summer. This really is a country fishing library if ever there was one.

Where should you start? All the twentieth-century greats are here in profusion: Falkus, Oglesby, Waddington, Menzies, Little, Graesser, Jock Scott, Dawson and of course the magnificent Ashley Cooper. For a while I look at the magnificiently bound copy of *The Great Salmon Rivers* but soon put it down. After all, what salmon fisher has not got all these editions himself – albeit not limited or signed or in perfect condition? It's the same with the American connection: Netboy, La Branche and Wulff are all up there, but I've read them before – every page – and I'm here for something new. (The copy of Wulff is really something special with plates hand-tinted by the author himself!)

Some Rarer Classics

I'm here, in large part anyway, to look at the first edition of Scrope's *Days and Nights of Salmon Fishing*, a copy signed two hundred years ago with a grand flourish. There cannot be a finer version anywhere in existence, and the frontispiece looks as though nobody has ever even thumbed it over the generations. The colours glow just as they must have done in the great man's day, when he picked the book up and reached for his quill to sign. You browse through and realize that some of his maxims are worthy of mention even today: 'Nobody should go into the water deeper than the fifth button of his waistcoat' (presumably we are counting from the top!), 'Throw clear beyond the spot where the salmon lies so that he may not see the fly light upon the water. Give him time to turn his head on his way back to his seat, to which a salmon always returns after rising to the fly. They never take well when the weather is about to change and if in dreams one relives the excitement of the river, who can blame him? At the dead hour of twelve I was awakened by loud cries of "I have him, I have him". "Hold him fast then", said I for I thought he had collared a thief but in truth he had not. He had only hold of the bellrope and was fishing away with it in his dreams with a salmon of course at the end of it!"

George Kelson

I was also told to look out for George Kelson's classic, *The Salmon Fly*, also signed and also with plates that glow with undiminished colour. What a man Kelson was – a true fly fisher – and just holding his book brings it all back. He was not just a fisherman but also a cricketer for Kent, and in 1871 scored four consecutive innings of 102, 101, 115 and 164 not out. He was a great salmon fisherman and reckoned on 4,000 captures in his life. He was the true all-rounder as well, the type of man that Falkus would applaud.

One season of his record book tells of captures of a twenty-four-pound pike, a $10\frac{1}{4}$-pound trout on bait, $9\frac{1}{4}$-pounder on fly, a $6\frac{3}{4}$-pound chub and an eleven-pound barbel! I can't think of many fisherman who could beat that today, especially when you add that he took sixty salmon from the Dee in three afternoons that same year! Rumour has it that he always wore a black bowler hat when he fished, in the frontispiece he sits resplendent in it. The hat served many purposes, and Kelson wound all his spare casts round and round it with loving care. Once, when he slipped and fell into the river, his only concern was that the hat should be scooped out of a bankside eddy

Faithfully yours
Geo. M. Kelson

The frontispiece of Kelson's famous book.

ingly, he spent as many warm days as possible actually sitting in the river, in the shallower salmon lies: 'We came to the conclusion that the stiller the surface of the water, the more favourable it is for inspection: but the brighter the day, so long as the sun is not in the background, the more clearly can the details and the conduct of the fly materials be scrutinized: that, however seemingly still the water may be, there is always a movement in some part of the fly, also, that to the human eye, a dark fly shows best on a dark day whilst in bright weather a fly of many colours is minutely distinguishable. This is not all. I benefited further for it taught me the grand lesson not to play long-hackled patterns which of themselves, unassisted by rod action, assume a lifelike motion even in the quietest water possible. I also learnt that a person talking on the bank can be heard by another underwater. Whether a fish can so hear is a question'. Kelson makes you understand why so many anglers just burn to write: they have so much in them that it has to come out on the page. Kelson, though, was a technician and a brilliant one.

Lord Grey
Lord Grey found something else in his fishing – an escape from the pressures of high-level public life, from the damaging knowledge that he was Foreign Secretary when the First World War was declared. Grey, like so many of us, was a country man forced into the city, an angling slob pushed into suits. Grey is the one who makes your heart sink. Look at these words: 'It is a great moment when, for the first time of the season, one stands by the side of a salmon river in early spring. The heart is full with the prospect for a whole season's sport. It is the beginning of a new angling year and the feel of the rod, the sound of the reel, the perpetual sight of moving water are all with one again after months of longing and absence. Every stream looks as if it must hold a salmon and if the salmon must rise and one begins to cast, trembling with excitement and eagerness'.

before it sank and all the work went to waste.

What I like about Kelson so much is that he was obviously a trier. He took nothing for granted, and he worked for every single thing that gave him pleasure. Above all he had to see things proved: 'Eminent scientists have told us how difficult it is even for a man of superior intelligence to keep distinct what he actually sees to what he thinks he sees. It is so very easy to see what agrees with one's own preconceived ideas'. This he applied exactingly to the salmon fly in the water. By his time, even, there were plenty of theories about what a salmon fly does in the water, but Kelson was determined to find out as far as he could for himself. Accord-

If an afternoon spent in the library shows

A sleepy Wessex river. The pipes keep away the midges.

just why anglers have to write, it also shows why others must collect. Gem after gem shouts out from the shelves. There is a copy of *A Man May Fish* with a dry fly on the cover under an eye of glass. There is a first edition of Halford's dry fly classic, signed of course with notes here and there in the pages by the author. A couple of his hand-tied dry flies are pressed between the pages and there are colour charts all the way through to show in the most minute detail the effects to be achieved. There is a first edition of Skues, again underlined here and there by the author with a few jokes at Halford's expense pencilled in.

Less Famous Works

There are some of the less well-known classics, like the Ernest E. Briggs copy of *Angling and Art in Scotland*. This must be one of the most

precious editions ever, with a little sermon of thanks on the title page to a generous host. Then there are all the books by the Braithwaites – one of the most extraordinary sporting families ever to fish salmon in Scotland. There was G. F. Braithwaite, the great-grandfather and then Cecil Braithwaite, the grandfather. Geoffrey Braithwaite, father, followed on, and Geoffrey Braithwaite, son, completed the sporting dynasty with possibly the best book of them all, *Happy Days with Rod, Gun and Bat*. (Notice that cricket creeps in again: The great salmon fishers were as much at home with willow as with cane! Did I tell you that Mowbray-Wells, the legendary Vosso salmon killer, twice bowled out W. G. Grace as well as playing rugby for England?)

You won't believe it, but my host comes in to ask me if I would care to stay for a spot of supper and talk literature. I look at the grand-

Heroic fish. Heroic angler.

father clock. It's a quarter to eight! Where on earth has the day gone, but how on earth could it have been better spent than delving in to the thoughts and the lives of heroes past?

ANGLING AND ART

Robin Armstrong

Now it's December, and for most anglers there's little to do but dream, read, think about past glories and anticipate delights to come. There are few people in the world who can help you along this road more surely than Robin

Armstrong. Robin, when I first met him, lived in an old cottage in a most secret Devonshire village. Even when you knew the address and found the place, you could be a long while from arriving at his door. The day I met him was a blisteringly hot one, and though it was early July the colours of the landscape had matured to give the look of August. Very shortly, we were where Robin wanted to be – down the hillside, walking in the shade of the valley along the river. We wandered miles, and a multitude of Robin Armstrongs came into my view.

First, I saw him as a water bailiff. Having now turned to full-time art, this job of a dozen years is not forgotten. He commented constantly on the state of the water-starved river. He knew the pools so intimately that he saw salmon when I barely even saw the water itself. He knew all the bed's depressions and the bankside undercuts and realized that poachers knew them also. A couple of snapped-off willow wands he discovered were poachers' rods. An area of long grasses flattened was a poacher's seat. A smidgeon of dried slime on a leaf showed that the poachers had caught fish.

Accompanying this bailiff's easy way along this waterbank was the long-acquired knowledge of a countryman and naturalist. He lamented an old and majestic pine debarked by cattle and doomed therefore to die. He often stopped to listen to a particular birdsong and to watch a butterfly or to observe the behaviour of the dragonflies. Over and above all these things, of course he showed that he is an angler. Pool by pool we stopped and he marked the fish: a six-pounder under a bank over there and a near fourteen-pounder at the tail of a weir. For each fish he worked out a strategy for the evening when dinner would be done, and we could fish for a couple of hours before the pub closed. For myself, I could hardly wait, but I saw the sense in his call for patience. It was his river, and he called its tune.

Above all things, however, I saw Robin Armstrong as an artist and realized just why his books are so acclaimed. He is fascinated by water as a substance. I watched him analyse it

Sheer majesty. John Russell's study of a 42½-pound cock salmon, painted before the pool of its capture, Banff's Rock, Forglen House.

as it flowed over stones and bubbled in the rapids and boiled in the little weirs. He pointed out how water holds and reflects light and how the surface film is an element that constantly changes under sun or cloud, breeze or calm, twilight or full day. We looked over a bridge. He pointed out the water running a couple of feet beneath thick alder leaves where the sun was striking here and there as the wind blew them back. Where the light hit the water, it turned opaque in an otherwise clear, dark stream. An insect fell and struggled to the surface, floating slowly downriver towards us. It came close. It was a wasp, and its legs and wings kicked out ripples that beat the water's film and cast rings of shadow on the gravel bed. A tiny moorland brown trout came up to it, nosed it, tugged and tore at it until finally it was no more. 'What a picture', Armstrong said.

It is such sights that Armstrong now wants to capture. His paintings have the feel of the water and portray it as it really is, as probably only anglers know it. Before Robin Armstrong, most – if not all – angling artists could be better described as illustrators. Water has been merely a background for their fish to be set upon and rarely existed in its own right. In Armstrong's paintings, the fish is merely a focal point and although brilliantly executed is almost dispensable. The water itself, the tricks it plays, and the moods it assumes are taking over an importance for him.

There's a great deal of excitement hanging about Robin's studio. This is pioneering stuff, and so there must be trepidation. There are a great many things that can and do go wrong. Some canvases lie overnight in a full bath to soak in water and gain a sheen. Fish and weeds of great intricacy are dowsed in washes of colour that could obliterate them and ruin days of work. The fear of failure, though, is nothing compared with the elation of success. This is why *The Painted Stream* and *Split Cane and Sable* have been such enormous successes.

Carving

Very recently, in a fishing hut on a Border river, well hidden by broken cane furniture and the accumulated gloom and debris of years, the carved, wooden salmon was seen. Perhaps a stray beam of sunlight chinked through the rafters to catch its eye, or perhaps it fell to the floor from its rusted nail and rotted rope. However, attention was drawn to it and the piece went off to be cleaned and polished. The caudal fin was chipped and a pectoral was broken clear off, but the carving was highly skilful, the fish that was its original model had been a large one and, when the carving went for sale, an enormous sum was paid for it.

Carvings of fish, generally Atlantic salmon, entered the art world from the late-Victorian period and dominated until the Second World War. The very best examples of this genre were finely worked and beautifully and realistically painted. They were copied from the actual fish with remarkable accuracy, and art really did mirror life itself. Mallock in Perth offered a service, and so, inevitably, did the Hardy brothers and Farlowe's. However, research by Simon and Edwina Brett suggests that the greatest of the creations came from the studio of John Russell, his daughter Isabella and her husband John Tully during the period 1819–1913. Simon has conducted an enormous amount of research into the art of model-

ling, and according to him it certainly seems that carved fish took precedence over stuffed fish during the last quarter of the nineteenth century. The most dramatic collection was owned by the Duke of Richmond and Gordon, who fished the Spey each autumn with his guests. Fish – at least the leviathans of over forty pounds – were immortalized in wood and swam seemingly eternally on the walls of the smoking room of the Duke's Scotland seat. How great was the beauty, how important that history, and how inspiring were the memories that glinted off those submarine bodies in the lamplight. Imagine their captors sitting beneath them, proven anglers, perhaps even great ones, looking through brandy glasses and cigar smoke at the opponents of their lives. In the silence the triumphs must have flooded back and resounded round the room. It is tragic for collectors, artists and fisherman that the collection is no more, that the fish were all destroyed by fire, and that the anglers who caught them are long since dead.

On a happier note, it is worth noting that Simon Brett now offers a modern fish-carving service. It took Simon and his wife some years to find an artist capable of reviving this lost art, but at last they located Roger Brookes, whose fine work more than qualifies him to continue the tradition. Should you be in any doubt, then a visit to the Brett's amazing and beautiful shop in Moreton-in-Marsh should settle any doubts

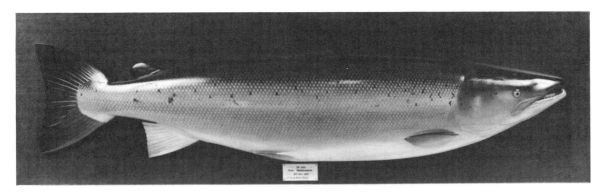

The beauty of a carved salmon.

What fisherman could resist the fascination of a shop like this?

that you might harbour. There will be at least one example of a modern carved salmon hanging there, and you will find it extremely beautiful – a worthy successor to the work of Russell and his family all those years ago.

Simon's shop is well worth a visit in any case because it helps explain the passion and the love that so many anglers have felt for salmon for so many decades. Salmon have inspired so much in so many, and the shop bears fulsome testimony to this: there you will find the most stunning collection of salmon fishing artifacts gathered from over the years. Magnificent rods, reels, flies, wallets, nets – everything to do with the business of salmon fishing is stacked there, talking to you of triumphs and tragedies from decades past.

NOTES

FINDING WHERE TO FISH

Probably the most straightforward way of finding salmon fishing is through the magazines, all of which carry a great many classified advertisements. *Salmon, Trout and Sea Trout, Trout and Salmon* and *Salmon and Trout* are all high-quality regular magazines which contain pages of excellent fishing potential. However, it is always wise to probe very carefully when you ring or write. Try to talk to the management, and make sure that there is a real knowledge there. All too often it is easy to book onto fishing where all the records are very vague; so try to get some idea of the annual records and the particular high spots each year. It could well be that only the really bad periods are for let.

Another good publication is the annual book *Fishing Forays* published by Kensington West Productions (Tel: 0434 609933). This is a very well-produced book, containing a great deal of information on game fishing possibilities around Great Britain. Obviously a great deal of research goes into making the book, and its advice can be trusted implicitly. Another excellent book is the long-term annual *Where to Fish*, now published by Thomas Harmsworth Publishing Company. This book has been in existence for decades and still contains a great deal of valid information. *The Salmon Rivers of Scotland* by Derek Mills and Neil Graesser, published by Ward Lock, is also an excellent guide to fishing north of the Border.

Both Savilles (the international property consultants) and Bidwells (Tel: 0463 715585) can offer advice on fishing to buy or to let on a long-term basis.

Finally, each year, the Atlantic Salmon Trust publishes a booklet of fishing that can be let by auction. These are often splendid and diverse (Tel: 0796 473439).

TACKLE

Perhaps I have concentrated on Hardy tackle too unfairly: there is obviously a great deal of excellent tackle on the market, and it would only be fair to mention Bruce and Walker in particular. Their rods have had a very strong following indeed, and if men like Arthur Oglesby endorse them, there can be nothing wrong at all. Contact them on 0487 813764 for their brochure. Grays of Alnwick have an equally fine reputation, and some of their rod designs are said to lead the field. Contact them on 0665 510020. By the way, the House of Hardy can be contacted on 0665 602771.

There are some excellent tackle shops, large and small, all round the country. Tom C. Saville Ltd has an excellent catalogue *The Game Fisherman*. This can be ordered from 0602 784248. The same can be said of Orvis UK Ltd and they can be contacted at The Mill, Nether Wallop, Stockbridge, Hants. Bob Church also makes excellent tackle for the game angler at a slightly less exotic price. The company's address is 16 Lorne Road, Northampton.

Still with the large concerns, I have often made a point of stopping in Perth on my way north at the Field Sports Shop. It is, as far as I am concerned, the gateway to Scottish sport! Contact them on 0738 441572.

Of course, shops do not have to be large to be exciting and helpful. Let me give you the example of Appleby Sports Supplies, The Market Place, Appleby, Cumbria. This is, or certainly was, run by the admirable Mr John Pape, and I well remember the advice he gave me, even though it was several years ago. It seemed to me than that this is the essence of the smaller tackle shop: a place run by a man of tremendous experience with the generosity to pass on what he knows. In this way the tackle business becomes far more than simply a commercial affair and moves into a different realm altogether.

Buying by mail order is now very popular. Possibly the quickest service and the largest stock in Great Britain is offered by Sportsfish, Hay on Wye, Wales.

FLY TYING

There can be few greater satisfactions than catching a salmon on a fly tied yourself. It is cheaper this way, and you can vary the dressing and pattern to suit yourself. This is very important if a sparse dressing is required, for example.

Many of the magazines carry advertisements for suppliers of fly tying materials. Some of the most comprehensive of these are Grahams (Tel: 0204 841337), Lureflash Products Ltd (Tel: 070 958 0081), Carrilon UK (Tel: 0777 703770), and J. Black (Tel: 0363 83655). All these suppliers have the most comprehensive of brochures.

There are, as you would expect, a great number of books on fly tying on the market at present, for example, Bob Church's *Guide to New Fly Patterns* (Crowood Press, 1993). Fly tying is virtually a sport unto itself and is just as popular as the actual fishing for many! There is now also a monthly magazine called *Fly Fishing and Fly Tying*, published by Game Fishing Publications Ltd, which is a must for the serious salmon fly tier. So too, eventually at least, would be membership of the Fly Fishers' Guild. Finally, just like casting, one lesson is worth ten thousand words, and several go-

ahead adult education committees have now instigated fly tying courses at different schools around the country in the evening. It could well be worth a telephone call to your local Education Office to check up on these. What better way to spend a January evening than tying a fly that will eventually catch you a silver, summer-run grilse?

COURSES

The Simon Gawesworth School of Fly Fishing is centred on the Woodford Bridge Hotel, Milton Damerel, Olsworthy, Devon, EX22 7LL. Simon can be contacted on 0805 23256 or at the hotel on 0409 261481. Simon's classes tend to be small, so tuition is on as individual a basis as possible. He offers two-, three-, five- and seven-day courses, catering for all levels of expertise. In particular he offers a three-day Spey casting course, which most potential salmon anglers are going to find very useful indeed.

Also in the south-west is the Arundell Arms, owned and managed by a well-known fly angler herself, Anne Voss-Bark. This excellent hotel offers the most superb accommodation and fishing of its own. It is the perfect place for a fishing and get-away-from-it-all-type holiday. The hotel also offers several different fishing courses, notably the advanced salmon casting course. This is a 1½-day course on salmon casting techniques, designed for the trout fisherman wishing to progress to salmon fishing or the salmon fisherman wishing to advance his casting skills. It is not really suitable for the complete newcomer to fly fishing, since the hotel assumes a certain knowledge of basic casting techniques. The course covers over-head, false, shooting line, roll, Spey and double-Spey casting and also techniques with fixed-spool reels and multiplier. The Arundell Arms also offers a fascinating and unique course on sea trout fishing (mostly at night) and also the very popular wild brown trout guided three-day weekend – wild fishing at its very best. Mrs Voss-Bark can be contacted on 0566 784666.

Probably the most intensive course of all is offered by the mighty Hugh Falkus on his own waters in the Lake District. Having witnessed Hugh at first hand, I don't think anyone who goes on the course will either forget it or regret it. Mr Falkus can be contacted at Crag Cottage, Ravensglass, Cumbria.

For many years Arthur Oglesby has been running his course at the Seafield Lodge Hotel, Grantown-on-Spey. I cannot imagine a more knowledgeable or engaging character than Arthur. His tremendous experience and warm generosity combine to make him the most ideal and whole-hearted of teachers. These are the longest established fishing courses in Britain and have set hundreds on the right road in the past. Arthur is now also running excellent trips abroad: I suggest you contact him for all he has to offer (Tel: 0904 627234).

A great deal of good reports have come from the Tweedside School of Game Angling, run by Derek Brown (Tel: 0721 729570). The course is based at Tweeddale, and lessons are held on secluded private beats of the river. Accommodation is available, and all the important techniques are taught to a very high standard indeed.

Two well-known writers also run courses, which I am sure will be quite excellent, certainly judging from the quality of their writing. You can contact Charles Bingham on 0822 613899 and Crawford Little on 0387 74207. Both of them offer tuition to anglers of differing abilities, and I'm quite sure anybody would feel quite confident under their care.

The Salmon and Trout Association has also moved into the arena and now offers Fishing with Celebrity holidays. You can now fish with Bill Currie and Ian Neale on the Spey, for example. I have long been an admirer of Mr Currie's books, and I am quite sure the whole flavour of the week would be excellent. Enquiries should be made to Debbie Creasy on 0622 682182.

I am reliably told that tuition is now available in the very far north of Scotland at the Assynt School of Fly Fishing. Knowing this part of the country as I do, I am quite sure these courses would be utterly memorable. They are based on the Inverlodge Hotel, an establishment I can speak for personally, and fishing is on the Inver and the Kirkcraig – both utterly superb rivers, full of holding pools and interest (Tel: 0571 4496).

I would also like to mention Tony Jones' excellent courses, on the River Wye and the River Tweed. His number is 0544 267804, and he really is a mine of information, both about the middle-Wye and the Tweed around Peebles. The mystery of Tony's life is why so many anglers will rent very expensive salmon fishing, spend a fortune on tackle and then spend so relatively little on how to use it. As he says, the untutored salmon angler with the fly whirling above his head is a danger to himself and to anybody watching. It is a miracle more boatmen aren't maimed for life. A few hours' or days' tuition gives anybody a real base to use and to build on; and good fly casting really does mean good fishing. Not only does it put more salmon on the bank, but it provides a lot more pleasure. Tony tells me that he has no secrets whatsoever, and that all the knowledge that he has built up over the years is available to his clients. However, he stresses that when it comes to salmon, everybody is a learner – even the teacher.

Finally, it is worth keeping an eye on the major county fairs: very often there are casting arenas where instructors will take you from the off, or put right your most obvious problems. If you are fairly confident already, this can be a fairly cheap and efficient way of perfecting your technique.

LURES

Probably the biggest collection of artificial spinners, plugs and lures for sale in the UK at the moment is offered by Chris and Sue Harris and it is well worth telephoning them on 0692

581208 to ask for their excellent catalogue. It is also worth noticing that they have recently produced a book called *The Encyclopaedia of Lures*, published by The Crowood Press. This details every type of lure the salmon angler is likely to want to experiment with. Another good contact is Gordon Griffiths of Flying 'C' fame (Tel: 0203 440859).

For those of you interested in making your own artificials, another Crowood book will have the information you need. It is written by Charlie Bettell and called *The Art of Lure Fishing*.

There are several points about spinning for salmon, possibly the most important being to ensure that the hooks are absolutely sharp. This is critical and it is well worth buying a sharpening stone and giving the hooks a quick once-over every time the lure is changed.

Many anglers also use leads on the line without really thinking the action through. For example, are leads actually necessary, and if so exactly how much weight should be put on the line and at what distance from the lure? It is also worth discovering if a weight substantially alters the lure's action, which in itself can be very detrimental.

Take great care with all swivels and snap links and check the leaders frequently for twists or abrasion. If pike are around, it is probably wise to use a wire trace. Otherwise, several lures can easily be lost to the sharp teeth of the big predator. Nothing is easier than making up a wire trace with crimps and pliers.

Most nylon lines come from Germany or Japan, and despite the different names on the spools, they nearly all come from the same source. However, there are new generations of lines beginning to appear, and the most notable is probably Corastrong, made by Cormorant. The gentlemen from Sport Fish in Hay say that they would now use no other line for their spinning on the Line. However, at £35 a spool this is not a cheap piece of tackle. Apparently, Leeda are soon to bring out a similar type of wire called Outcast. This, too, is likely to be expensive but offers great advantages in strength, thinness and resilience. Presumably the prices will come down gradually, and spinning techniques will be able to make another leap into the future.

FISHING IN IRELAND

If you are thinking of visiting Ireland for salmon fishing, there are a few important things to remember. You must get a State Licence for salmon fishing anywhere. This costs the magnificent sum of £25 – very reasonable for a whole year's fishing. Before you travel, it is advisable to contact the Fisheries Office in Dublin (Tel: 01 379 206), as it will give you any up-to-date information on catches and river conditions. It also pays to keep an eye on all the magazine reports and study the monthly catch returns.

Ireland has a few airports, and Dublin is the major one, but use Ryan Air to fly to Knock Airport in Co. Mayo. Cork Airport is also handy for fishing in the south.

As for tackle, a fourteen-foot double-handed fly rod and a smaller ten- to eleven-foot trout fly rod will be all you need. However, it would be wise to bring a good spinning rod as well, certainly for early-season work. If you can, bring a dapping rod for the lakes if they are to be your base. A reel loaded with two hundred yards of backing and a few yards of floss will be fine for this. Make sure the rod is at least fourteen feet in length. You could even use a double-handed fly rod to dapp; but these are rather awkward and heavier than telescopic dapping rods made specifically for the purpose. Never forget to bring or hire a life-jacket, for the Irish lakes are very large, wild places.

The Irish Tourist Board Angling Representative is a man called Paul Harris, and he is invariably informative and knowledgeable. He can be contacted on 0788 833203.

Ireland, of course, inspires literature and I would recommend some essential reading:

The Trout and Salmon Loughs of Ireland by Peter O'Reilly

The Angler in Ireland by Ken Whealon

The Wild Sports of the West of Ireland by W. H. Maxwell

A Gamefisher in Ireland by Colin McElvie

A Man May Fish by T. C. Kingsmill Moore.

FISHING IN NORWAY

I have been told that probably the wisest way to fish in Norway is simply to get yourself over there, get hold of a car and drive off into the countryside, asking as you go. Providing you have sufficient funds and enough confidence, it is possible that good fishing will come your way. However, I am well aware that holidays are treasured times, and you do not want to leave anything to chance.

My contacts in Germany tell me that Manfred Raguse is the man to contact. He has recently completed a video called *Fly Fishing in Norway*, which apparently is very helpful indeed. He is also a prime mover in the Norwegian Fly Fishers' Club, which can arrange fishing in that country. He can be contacted on 010 49 40 4302529. His UK representative is Stuart Townsley and he can be contacted on 0289 382074.

A true expert on Norwegian fishing is Tarquin Millington-Drake. He is often very generous with his advice and even his contacts. He can be contacted through Ker and Downey, 14 Old Bond Street, London WIX 3DD.

Whilst talking about Norwegian salmon fishing, it makes sense to mention Iceland. The Ranga fished especially well in the early 1990s, and the Angling Service, Strengir in Reykjavic, is apparently quite helpful. Their number is 354 1 687090. Their fax number is 354 1 678122 (I give their fax number, as faxing is often preferable to phoning when you are dealing at long distance). Iceland Air is also moving into the salmon fishing holiday area, and they can be contacted on 071 388 5599.

FISHING IN RUSSIA

Salmon fishing in Russia is now really big business, with many different firms moving into the frame. In this country, Kola Salmon Ltd in Hungerford seems to be taking a lot of people over there. It can be contacted on 0488 683222. UK Field and Stream (Tel: 0527 66344) and Nimrod Safaris Ltd (Tel: 0285 810132) also offer trips to the Kola.

Probably the biggest mover in foreign fishing holidays is Finlayson Hughes up in Scotland. This company really is building up a vast reputation for some of the most exotic fishing, and Russia has been in its catalogue now for some years, so it must be ironing out any of the wrinkles. You will also find that this company is able to help on Norway, Iceland and anywhere you might conceivably want to fish. Contact them on 0738 30926.

With all these companies about you might feel in need of some independent advice, and Barlows in London is pleased to offer this. Contact the company on 071 839 2423.

It just might pay to think about travelling to the Kola with one of the foreign companies who have operated there before the British got into the field. I have personal knowledge of Outdoor East, a Swedish company run by Johan Abelsson. In fact, I travelled with him to southern Russia and the arrangements were impeccable. I suspect his tours to the north are just the same. Contact him on 010 46 86 50 1754. Exactly the same goes for Beluga Tours run by Michael Reiter. He can be contacted in Germany on 010 49 64 225822 (fax 010 4964 6046). His English is absolutely excellent, and his knowledge is extensive.

COLLECTORS' BOOKS

Collecting old books on salmon fishing is quite a joy in itself but there are traps for the unwary. Wherever possible, try to make sure that you are buying a first edition. There are exceptions to this rule (for example with *The Compleat*

Angler), but mostly collectors go for the first edition, and money can be wasted on others. The condition is absolutely vital. Check particularly that illustrations and plates have not been removed to be framed. Obviously, if the book ever had a dust jacket, it is more valuable if that is in place and in good condition too. Finally, it is always nice to have associated copies (these are copies that are linked with the author in some special way). Perhaps the book will have been signed, possibly with some message. The book might even have been owned by a famous angler or there might be notes in it made by the author. Letters, too, can sometimes be found in a book and increase its value.

It is always advisable to buy from reputable dealers, and you can be quite sure that none of these listed below will make unreasonable charges.

John Scott Sporting Books (Tel: 0299 896779)
Coch-y-Bonddu (Tel: 0654 702837)
John and Judith Head (Tel: 0722 327767)
Major Iain Grahame, Dawes Hall, Lamarsh, Bures, Suffolk
Simon Gough, Fish Hill, Holt, Norfolk.

ANGLING ARTEFACTS

I have already mentioned Simon Brett, and it is wise to phone him before making a visit to his shop. He is available on 0608 50751.

A great many angling artefacts are available through various auctions, and these days the biggest and most frequent of these are operated by Neil Freeman. I have known Neil for some time, and he has bought and sold things for me in a most efficient and honourable way! Through his previous employments, Neil has a great deal of experience in the area and can advise expertly. He is available on 081 749 4175.

Bonhams have a highly respected name in this field also. They have at least one major auction of angling objects (Tel: 071 548 9161). North of the border, Christies operates from Glasgow, and its annual sale is a much-awaited event. Contact the company on 031 225 4756.

It can be worth contacting some of the private dealers if you are searching for a specific object or if you have something that you think is valuable to sell. One of the most high-profile of these dealers – and one about whom I've heard good reports – is Jamie Maxtone-Graham. He is certainly a man of great knowledge and is generally willing to help. He is available on 0721 740304.

The modern definitive book on angling and art was recently produced by Tom Quinn, and Bernard Venables' life story also provides a fascinating insight into how an angler and paintbrush work in harmony. The book is published by Merlin Unwin and is called *The Illustrated Memoirs of a Fisherman*. Two other artists well worth looking out for are Chris Turnbull and John Searle. Both are comparatively young artists, producing a great deal of high-quality work. Both are available for commissions: contact John on 0425 655663 and Chris on 0603 632187.

INDEX